18TH CENTURY RECORDS *of the* GERMANTOWN REFORMED CHURCH *of* PENNSYLVANIA

F. Edward Wright

HERITAGE BOOKS
2022

HERITAGE BOOKS
AN IMPRINT OF HERITAGE BOOKS, INC.

Books, CDs, and more—Worldwide

For our listing of thousands of titles see our website
at
www.HeritageBooks.com

Published 2022 by
HERITAGE BOOKS, INC.
Publishing Division
5810 Ruatan Street
Berwyn Heights, Md. 20740

— Publisher's Notice —
Pages 37 to 44 are missing.

International Standard Book Number
Paperbound: 978-0-7884-2598-1

INTRODUCTION

George Michael Weiss organized a Reformed congregation in Germantown ca. 1727. He was followed by John Peter Miller (1730-1731), John Bartholomew Rieger (1731-1734) and John Bechtel at various times between 1728 and 1744. In 1732 the land was purchased for contruction of a church. By 1739 a church had been built. At the end of 1746, Michael Schlatter became pastor of the Philadelphia and Germantown congregations. He served the Germantown congregation until 1750. He was followed by John Conrad Steiner (1750-1756), John William Stoy (1756-1758), who served in Germantown and Philadelphia, John George Alsentz (1758-1767), John Christopher Faber (1767-1768), Christian Friederich Faehring (1769-1772), J. C. Albert Helffenstein (1772-1776) of Mosbach in the Palatinate, Casper Wack (supply in 1776), Samuel Dubendorff (1777-1779), J. C. Albert Helffenstein (1779-1790 and L. Frederick Herman (1790-1801).

The register was a "large, leather bound folio volume, 12 x 8 1/4 inches in size," containing 836 pages, many of which are blank.

F. Edward Wright
Westminster, Maryland
1994

GERMANTOWN REFORMED CHURCH
Now Market Square Presbyterian Church

Baptisms by the Rev. John Conrad Steiner, 1753 - 1756

1753

Dorothea, daughter of John Conrad Steiner, pastor loci, and Regula, nee Hegner, b. ----, bapt. January 1, 1753, died January 10. Spon: Henry Schellenberg and wife Dorothea.

Elizabeth, daughter of John Zacharias and Catharine, b. ----, bapt. January 7, 1753. Spon: George Dannehauer and wife.

Conrad, son of Jacob Mercki and Barbara, b. ----, bapt. January 14, 1753. Spon: Conrad Cramer and wife.

Dietrich (Deatrick), son of Dietrich Straubel and Elizabeth, Luth., b. ----, bapt. January 28, 1753. Spon: Daniel Grueninger and wife Barbara.

Anna Maria, daughter of Jacob Kloeti and Anna Maria, b. ----, bapt. February 4, 1753. Spon: Balthasar Dogy, Anna Maria Welklin, Anna Maria Baetschin.

Casper, son of Jacob Guettinger and wife, b. ----, bapt. February 11, 1753. Spon: Casper Sorber and wife.

Susanna, daughter of Rudolf Guettinger and Anna, b. ----, bapt. February 11, 1753. Spon: Rudolf Peter and Susanna Hoffmann.

John Gabriel, son of Abraham Salomon, dec. and Maria Elizabeth, b. ----, bapt. February 1, 1753. Spon: John Gabriel von Erden.

Elizabeth, daughter of Rudolf Naeff and Anna, b. ----, bapt. February 11, 1753. Spon: John Nuessli and wife Margaret.

Henry, son of John Bucher and Catharine, b. ----, bapt. February 12, 1753. Spon: Henry Schellenberg and wife Dorothy.

Andrew, son of Andrew Weckesser, Luth. and wife Ref., b. ----, bapt. February 19, 1753. Spon: Parents.

John George, son of John Tranck and Anna Elizabeth, b. ----, bapt. February 25, 1753. Spon: John George Schulz and wife Juliana.

John George, son of George Bloch and Anna Elizabeth, b. ----, bapt. February 25, 1753. Spon: Martin Jost.

Jacob, son of Joseph Staeheli and Anna Maria Veronica, b. ----, bapt. March 4, 1753. Spon: Jacob Kübler and Anna Schwenck.

John, son of Valentine Klages and Elizabeth, b. ----, March 18, 1753. Spon: John Sorber and his mother Anna Maria.

Elizabeth, daughter of Charles Widerhold and Susanna, b. February 19, 1753, March 18, 1753. Spon: The father and Barbara Widman.

A child of John Haag, Luth. and Anna Margaret, b. ----, March 19, 1753. Spon: ----.

Catharine, daughter of Leonard Froeli and Catharine, b. ----, bapt. March 25, 1753. Spon: Jacob Rumen and wife Catharine.

Catharine Barbara, daughter of Jacob Werner and Anna Maria, Luth., b. ----, bapt. April 7, 1753. Spon: Jacob Binder and Catharine Barb. Kopp.

Anna Barbara, daughter of Martin Schlotter and Anna Barbara, Luth., b. ----, bapt. April 16, 1753. Spon: George Philip Reiber and wife Anna.

Michael Christopher, son of Henry Sumerer and Veronica, b. ----, bapt. April 20, 1753. Spon: Michael Christopher Hauser and wife Regula, Luth.

Matthias, son of Theobold Peyer and wife, b. ----, bapt. April 22, 1753. Spon: Matthias Gaensel, Luth. and wife.

John, son of Jacob Schuster and Anna Eva, b. February 25, 1753, bapt. April 22, 1753. Spon: John Adam and Anna Barbara.
An English child John, of ----, b. ----, bapt. April 22, 1753. Spon: ----.
A child of Jacob Rau and wife, b. ----, bapt. April 23, 1753. Spon: William Hoffman and wife.
Jacob, son of Jacob Hegi and Maria, b. ----, bapt. May 10, 1753. Spon: Parents.
John Jacob, son of Conrad Kramer and Anna, b. ----, bapt. May 13, 1753. Spon: Jacob Meyer and wife Anna.
Anna Maria, daughter of Henry Dippel and Catharine, b. ----, bapt. May 20, 1753. Spon: Henry Scherfler and wife Anna Maria.
Jacob, son of Christian Geisler and Sarah, b. ----, bapt. June 11, 1753. Spon: Parents.
A black child of ----, b. ----, bapt. August 19, 1753. Spon: ----.
Margaret, daughter of John Woffeckert and Joanna, b. ----, bapt. August 26, 1753. Spon: Sebastian Mueller and wife Margaret.
Maria Louisa, daughter of Henry Meyer and wife, b. ----, bapt. September 2, 1753. Spon: John Unverzagt and wife Maria Louisa, Luth.
John, son of John Peter Weiss and Magdalene, b. ----, bapt. September 23, 1753. Spon: Michael Weiss and wife Anna Catharine.
Abraham, son of Felix Gerdun and Eva, b. ----, bapt. September 30, 1753. Spon: Abraham N. (unknown) and Margaret.
Elizabeth, daughter of Herman Orner and Margaret, b. ----, bapt. September 30, 1753. Spon: Conrad and Catharine Schuez.
William, son of John Bergerhof and Anna, b. ----, bapt. September 30, 1753. Spon: The father and Margaret Orner.
Jacob, son of Henry Baer and Verena, b. ----, bapt. September 30, 1753. Spon: Jacob Baer and Barbara Krauer.
Maria Margaret, daughter of Peter Schirmer and Magdalene, b. ----, bapt. October 7, 1753. Spon: Abraham and Margaret Betillon.
A child of Abraham Heinrich and wife, b. ----, bapt. October 14, 1753. Spon: ----.
Anna Catharine, daughter of John Bergerhoff and wife, b. ----, bapt. October 21, 1753. Spon: Conrad Schuez and wife Catharine.
John Conrad, son of Conrad Ruesch and Catharine, b. ----, bapt. October 21, 1753. Spon: Conrad Nauber.
A newcomer of ----, b. ----, bapt. October 28, 1753. Spon: --.
Catharine, daughter of Leonard Froeli and Catharine, b. ----, bapt. November 18, 1753. Spon: Jacob Rumen and wife Catharine.
Barbara, daughter of Henry Mercki and Barbara, b. ----, bapt. November 18, 1753. Spon: Casper Sorber and wife Barbara.
John Philip, son of John Philip Sulzbach and wife, b. ----, bapt. November 19, 1753. Spon: John Herman Dippel and wife Catharine.
John, son of Jacob Meyer and Anna, b. ----, bapt. December 16, 1753. Spon: John Krauer and wife Regula.
Verena, daughter of Ulrich Weidman and Anna, b. ----, bapt. December 23, 1753. Spon: Ulrich Zollinger and wife Verena.
Maria Elizabeth, daughter of Jacob Waser and Anna Barbara, b. ----, bapt. December 23, 1753. Spon: Michael Dieter and wife Maria

Elizabeth.

Anna Catharine, daughter of Christian Schmit and Cath. Elizabeth Becker, illegitimate, bapt. December 26, 1753. Spon: John William Becker and wife Anna Eva.

1754

John George, son of John Philip Schneider and Anna Catharine, b. ----, bapt. January 13, 1754. Spon: George Kaerst and wife Elizabeth.

John Gottfried (Godfrey), son of Christopher Beck and Elizabeth, b. ----, bapt. January 13, 1754. John Gottfried Somerlad and wife Maria Cath.

John George, son of John George Bickis and Barbara, b. ----, bapt. February 3, 1754. Spon: John George Bouton and Miss Elizabeth Haag (Maag?).

Henry, son of John Michel and Barbara, b. ----, bapt. February 17, 1754. Spon: Henry Reinhardt and wife Juliana.

Francis William, daughter of Gottfried Bokius and Philippina Cathar., b. ----, bapt. March 13, 1754. Spon: Francis Wilhelm.

Anna Maria, daughter of John Goezelman and Christine, b. ----, bapt. March 14, 1754. Spon: Anna Maria wife of Michael Kachel.

Mary Magdalene, daughter of John David Seifenfeld and Maria Barbara, Luth., b. ----, bapt. March 14, 1754. Spon: Andrew Stahl and wife Anna Magdalene.

Elizabeth, daughter of William Hoffman and wife, b. ----, bapt. March 17, 1754. Spon: Henry Reinhart and wife Juliana.

Anna, daughter of John Rudolf Maurer and Anna Landis, b. ----, bapt. March 17, 1754. Spon: Rudolf Mauerer and Anna Mueller, his wife.

Daniel, son of Jacob Rebol and Louise, b. ----, bapt. March 17, 1754. Spon: Daniel Benezet and wife.

John Jacob, son of Michael Conrad and Catharine, b. ----, bapt. March 17, 1754. Spon: John Jacob Conrad and wife Regula.

Margaret, daughter of Nicholas Rehbein and Margaret, b. ----, bapt. March 25, 1754. Spon: Parents.

Elizabeth, daughter of Jacob Gallmann and Elizabeth, b. ----, bapt. March 25, 1754. Spon: Parents.

John, son of Felix Dutweiler and Elizabeth, b. ----, bapt. April 1, 1754. Spon: John Sorber and Anna Schwenck.

John Frederick, son of Christopher Heller and Catharine, Luth., b. ----, bapt. April 1, 1754. Spon: John Gruenewald and wife Elizabeth.

Maria Catharine, daughter of Christian Rick and Elizabeth, Luth., b. ----, bapt. April 1, 1754. Spon: George Henry Koop and wife Anna Maria.

Anna Maria, daughter of Jacob Fischer and Juliana, Luth., b. ----, bapt. April 6, 1754. Spon: Parents.

Elizabeth, daughter of Daniel Haubensack and Eleonora Juliana, b. ----, bapt. April 9, 1754. Spon: Adam Heider and Elizabeth.

John Henry, son of John Nebel and Marianna, Luth., b. ----, bapt. April 14, 1754. Spon: Henry Schuessler and wife Catharine.

Jacob, son of John Seiler and Anna Catharine, b. ----, bapt. April 14, 1754. Spon: Jacob Koenig and wife Juliana.

Barbara, daughter of Henry Sumerer and wife Veronica, b. ----, bapt. April 15, 1754. Spon: John George Bickis and wife

Barbara.

John William, son of William Stadelman and Catharine, Luth., b. ----, bapt. April 15, 1754. Spon: Nicholas Lochmann and Elizabeth Hey.

Catharine, daughter of Gottfried Tauenhauer and Anna Catharine, b. ----, bapt. April 24, 1754. Spon: John Mueller and Catharine Herlacher.

Anna Maria, daughter of Conrad Schuez and Catharine, b. ----, bapt. April 28, 1754. Spon: Henry Bassler and wife Anna Maria.

Anna, daugther of John Stein and Eliabeth Truebin, illegitimate, bapt. April 28, 1754. Spon: Leonard Froeli and Anna Kramer.

Magdalene, daughter of Ulrich Freyhofer and Magdalene, b. ----, bapt. May 9, 1754. Spon: Parents.

Henry, son of Jacob Rüeg and Barbara, b. ----, bapt. May 9, 1754. Spon: Parents.

Susanna, daughter of Stephen Gneisen and Catharine, Luth., b. ----, bapt. May 12, 1754. Spon: Susanna Magdalene Pfeiffer.

Jacob, son of Jacob Weidman and Susanna, b. ----, bapt. May 19, 1754. Spon: Jacob Weidman, grandfather and wife Regina.

Francis, daughter of Jean Bigonet and Catharine Elizabeth, b. ----, bapt. May 19, 1754. Spon: Parents.

Jacob, son of Conrad Künzli and Barbara Illin, illegitimate, bapt. May 23, 1754. Spon: Jacob Fischer and Susanna Hoffmann.

Maria Rosina, daughter of Andrew Stahel and Anna Magdalene, b. ---, bapt. May 26, 1754. Spon: ----.

John Peter, son of Michael Simon and wife, b. ----, bapt. May 31, 1754. Spon: Parents.

George Ludwig (Lewis), son of Ludwig Gass and Maria Susanna, b. ----, bapt. June 2, 1754. Spon: John George Gass and wife Maria Susanna.

Henry, son of Conrad Maurer and Susanna, b. ----, bapt. June 2, 1754. Spon: Henry Baer and wife Verena.

Ulrich, son of Frederick Foth and Anna Margaret, b. ----, bapt. June 3, 1754. Spon: Ulrich Zollinger and wife Verena.

Anna Maria, daughter of Jacob Hess and Elizabeth, b. ----, bapt. June 9, 1754. Spon: Jacob Meyer and wife Anna Maria.

Maria Catharine, daughter of Henry Weidner and Catharine Elizabeth, b. ----, bapt. June 9, 1754. Spon: Martin Gruen and wife Catharine Elizabeth.

Anna Barbara, daughter of John Martin Foster and Helena Catharine, b. ----, bapt. June 9, 1754. Spon: Jacob Griess and wife Anna Barbara.

Jacob, son of Jacob Mercki and Barbara, b. ----, bapt. June 23, 1754. Spon: Jacob and Anna Meyer.

Anna, daughter of Rudolf Maurer and Anna, b. ----, bapt. June 28, 1754. Spon: Rudolf Maurer and wife Anna.

Ernest Jacob, son of George Paul Langenbach and Elizabeth, b. ----, bapt. July 14, 1754. Spon: Ernest Jacob Depeyer and wife Maria Agnes.

Sarah, daughter of Christian Geisler and Sarah, b. ----, bapt. August 25, 1754. Spon: Parents.

Mary Magdalene, daughter of Michael Baumann and wife, b. ----, bapt. August 26, 1754. Spon: Mary Magdalene Grueninger.

A child of John Fortmeyer and Margaret, b. ----, bapt. September 1, 1754. Spon: ----.

Theobald, son of Theobald Moll and Eva Margaret, b. ----, bapt. September 1, 1754. Spon: Parents.

Isaac and Jacob, sons of Jacob Kloeti and Maria, b. ----, bapt. September 5, 1754. Spon: Maria Leebruck.

John Philip, son of John Gerlach Lorniter and Catharine, b. ----, bapt. September 15, 1754. Spon: John Philip Bul and Elizabeth Rigg.

John Herman, son of John Peter Dippel and Magdalene, b. ----, bapt. September 22, 1754. Spon: John Hermand Dippel and wife Catharine.

John and Dorothea, son and daughter of ----, b. ----, bapt. September 22, 1754. Spon: John Schad and wife Adelheid.

Elizabeth Barbara, daughter of George Kiemer and Magdalene, Luth., b. ----, bapt. September 22, 1754. Spon: Theobald Peyer and Elizabeth Barbara.

John Jacob, son of Rudolf Sorber and Anna Maria, b. ----, bapt. September 29, 1754. Spon: Casper Sorber and wife Anna Barbara.

John Bernard, son of Conrad Schauegger and Agnes, b. ----, bapt. October 3, 1754. Spon: Jacob Gaensel and wife Catharine.

John Michael, son of Michael Letterli and Dorothea, b. ----, bapt. October 6, 1754. Spon: Ludwig Friz and wife Anna Maria.

Henry, son of John Conrad Steiner, pastor loci, and Regula, nee Hegner, b. ----, bapt. October 13, 1754. Spon: Henry Schellenberg and wife Dorothea.

Maria Martha, daughter of Valentine Klages and Elizabeth, b. ----, bapt. October 13, 1754. Spon: Martin Grüen and wife Maria Martha.

Anna Sophia, daughter of Jacob Bach and Maria Catharine, b. ----, bapt. October 20, 1754. Spon: Michael Renhert and wife Anna Sophia.

Anna Dorothea, daughter of David Kittler and Maria Elizabeth, b. ----, bapt. October 20, 1754. Spon: ----.

Catharine, daughter of Gottfried Sommerlad and Maria Catharine, Luth., b. ----, bapt. October 20, 1754. Spon: Christopher Beck and wife Elizabeth.

Verena, daughter of Peter Zollinger and Verena, b. ----, bapt. October 27, 1754. Ulrich Zollinger and wife Verena.

Anna Margaret, daughter of John Adam Hoh and Anna Margaret, b. ---, bapt. November --, 1754. Spon: Jacob Engler and wife Anna Margaret.

Hartman, son of George Leithäuser and Margaret, b. ----, bapt. November 17, 1754. Spon: Hartman Adam and wife.

John, son of Jacob Meyer and Anna, b. ----, bapt. December 8, 1754. Spon: Grandfather and wife Catharine.

Anna Margaret, daughter of Jacob Griess and wife, b. ----, bapt. December 10, 1754. Spon: William Hoffman and wife.

Jacob, son of Henry Isler and Anna, b. ----, bapt. December 15, 1754. Spon: Jacob Zibeli and Anna Duttweiler.

John Henry, son of William Truemper and Magdalene, b. ----, bapt. December 15, 1754. Spon: Parents.

John, son of William Truber and Anna Margaret, b. ----, bapt. December 22, 1754. Spon: John Meffert.

Anna Maria, daughter ofJohn Metzler and Christine, b. ----, bapt. December 26, 1754. Spon: Jean Toulisan and wife Anna Maria.

Barbara, daughter of Rudolf Guettinger and Anna, b. ----, bapt. December 29, 1754. Spon: Jacob Fischer and Barbara Kuebler.
Henry, son of Henry Schellenberg and Dorothea, b. ----, bapt. December 29, 1754. Spon: Parents.

1755
John George, son of John Binder and Elizabeth, b. ----, bapt. January 1, 1755. Spon: John George Binder and Magdalene Weidman.
Sarah, daughter of Peter Richter and Susanna, b. ----, bapt. January 16, 1755. Spon: Conrad Schuetz and wife Catharine.
Leonard, son of Ulrich Lanz and Maria Catharine, b. ----, bapt. February 2, 1755. Spon: Leonard Froeli and Anna Kramer.
Anna Elizabeth, daughter of George Reichwein and Susanna, b. ----, bapt. February 2, 1755. Spon: Jacob Han and wife Anna.
Anna Maria, daughter of Jacob Rau and wife, b. ----, bapt. February 16, 1755. Spon: William Hoffmann and wife Anna Maria.
John, son of Henry Naeff and Hannah, b. ----, bapt. February 16, 1754. Spon: John Eberli and wife Margaret.
Dorothy Elizabeth, daughter of Peter Meister and Sophia, b. ----, bapt. February 16, 1754. Spon: Dorothy Elizabeth Neuhardt.
Catharine, daughter of Peter Schirmer and Magdalene, b. ----, bapt. March 2, 1755. Spon: Abraham Betillion and wife Margaret.
Christopher, son of John Bokius and Elizabeth, b. ----, bapt. March 30, 1755. Spon: Christopher Keller and wife.
Rudolf, son of Jacob Maurer and Anna, b. ----, bapt. March 31, 1755. Spon: Rudolf Schuetz and wife Regula.
Barbara, daughter of George Bloch and Anna Elizabeth, b. ----, bapt. March 31, 1755. Spon: Barbara Walter.
John Herman, son of John Wolfeckert and Joanna, b. ----, bapt. March 31, 1755. Spon: John Herman Kellerman and Barbara.
Elizabeth, daughter of Samuel Neuschwander and Adelheid, b. ----, bapt. April 18, 1755. Spon: Parents.
John, son of Henry Baer and Verena, b. ----, bapt. May 4, 1755. Spon: Jacob Maurer and Anna Maurer.
Margaret, daughter of Herman Orner and A. Margaret, b. ----, bapt. May 18, 1755. Spon: Jacob Calman and wife Eva Maria.
Anna, daughter of Martin Grieder and Magdalene, b. ----, bapt. May 18, 1754. Spon: Jacob Naeff and Anna Buser.
Nicholas, son of John Bergerhof and wife, b. ----, bapt. June 15, 1755. Spon: Nicholas Rehbein and wife Margaret.
A negro child of ----, b. ----, bapt. June 19, 1755. Sponsors at Schellenberg's.
Anna Catharine, daughter of Peter Meyer and Judith, b. ----, bapt. June 22, 1755. Spon: Anna Cath. Hergesheimer.
Anna, daughter of Henry Koch and Margaret, b. ----, bapt. June 22, 1755. Spon: Jacob Pfeiffer and Anna Graf.
Maria, daughter of ---- Buechi and wife, b. ----, bapt. July 18, 1755. Spon: Parents.
Elizabeth, daughter of John George Bickis and Barbara, b. ----, bapt. July 27, 1755. Spon: John George Bouton and wife Elizabeth.
John Henry, son of John Jacob Sorber and Anna, b. ----, bapt. August 3, 1755. Spon: John Casper Sorber and wife Barbara.
Anna, daughter of Jacob Ebrecht and Elizabeth, b. ----, bapt.

August 17, 1755. Spon: Rudolf Ebrecht and Anna Ebrecht.

Rudolf, son of Jacob Guettinger and Verena, b. ----, bapt. August 17, 1755. Spon: Rudolf Weiss and wife Anna.

Regula, daughter of Frederick Lorenz and Anna, b. ----, bapt. August 17, 1755. Spon: Jacob Conrad and wife Regula.

Verena, daughter of Jacob Hauser and Anna, b. ----, bapt. August 17, 1755. Spon: Verena Wuerzler and Rudolf Zoebeli.

Maria, daughter of John Roth and Anna, b. ----, bapt. September 21, 1755. Spon: Parents.

John, son of Jacob Hegi and Maria, b. ----, bapt. November 2, 1755. Spon: Jacob Steiner and Barbara Widman.

Anna Elizabeth, daughter of Herman Dippel and wife, b. ----, bapt. November 16, 1755. Spon: Anna Elizabeth Tranck.

George Felix, son of Felix Gertun and wife, b. ----, bapt. November 16, 1755. Spon: George Felix Beck and wife.

Ulrich, son of Peter Zollinger and wife, b. ----, bapt. November 27, 1755. Spon: Ulrich Zollinger and wife Verena.

John Peter, son of John Peter Leeman and Maria Esther, b. ----, bapt. November 30, 1755. John George Bachofen and Anna Maria Kloeti.

Elizabeth, daughter of Abraham Betillion and Maria Margaret, b. ----, bapt. December 14, 1755. Spon: Dewald Diel and wife Magdalene.

Maria Christine, daughter of Conrad Neuhard and Dorothy Elizabeth, b. ----, bapt. December 14, 1755. Spon: Henry Bleker and Maria Christine Kein.

Jacob, son of Carl Wiethold and Susanna, b. October 19, 1755, bapt. December 14, 1755. Spon: Jacob Hegi and wife Anna Maria.

1756

John Peter, son of John Jacob Finchel and Christine, b. ----, bapt. January 1, 1756. Spon: John Peter Tranck.

Jacob, son of Leonard Froeli and Catharine, b. ----, bapt. January 11, 1756. Spon: Jacob Rumen and wife Catharine.

Dorothea, daughter of Paulus Geisel and Margaret, b. ----, bapt. January 27, 1756. Spon: Michael Neiz and Dorothea Meurin.

John, son of John Sorber and Anna, b. ----, bapt. January 27, 1756. Spon: Felix Duttweiler and wife Elizabeth.

Henry, son of Jacob Kern and Catharine, b. ----, bapt. February --, 1756. Spon: Jacob Greiss and wife Maria.

A child of (Henry) Naeff and wife, b. ----, bapt. February 3, 1756. Spon: ----.

A child of Jean Bigonet and Catharine Elizabeth, b. ----, bapt. February 8, 1756. Spon: Parents.

Susanna Magdalene, daughter of Jacob Baer and Barbara, b. ----, bapt. February 22, 1756. Spon: Jacob Weidman and wife Susanna.

Catharine, daughter of Peter Weiss and Anna Catharine, b. ----, bapt. March 8, 1756. Spon: Anna Catharine Weiss, the mother.

Anna Maria, daughter of Samuel Basemann and Judith, b. ----, bapt. March 8, 1756. Spon: Jean Toullisan and wife Anna Maria.

A child of Rudolf Ebrecht and Apollonia, b. ----, bapt. March 28, 1756. Spon: ----.

Frederick, son of Frederick Foth and Anna Margaret, b. ----, bapt. March 28, 1756. Spon: Ulrich Zollinger and wife Verena.

Anna Maria, daughter of George Fries and Anna Maria, b. ----, bapt.

March 28, 1756. Spon: ----.
John Philip, son of Philip Schneider and Anna Catharine, b. ----, bapt. May 1, 1756. Spon: Dewald Diller and Magdalene.
Catharine Margaret, daughter of John Seibold and Elizabeth, b. ----, bapt. May 1, 1756. Spon: Anna Margaret Leibold.
Gottfried, son of Jacob Supp and Anna Maria, b. ----, bapt. May 1, 1756. Gottfried Schmelzer and wife Catharine.
Henry, son of Gottfired Wilkin and Christine, b. ----, bapt. May 5, 1756. Spon: John George Wilkin and Susanna Basler.
Samuel, son of John Jost and Dorothea, b. ----, bapt. May 5, 1756. Spon: Jacob Maag and mother of child.
A child of Christian Geisler and Sarah, b. ----, bapt. June 6, 1756. Spon: Parents.

Baptisms by the Rev. John William Stoy
December 1756 - December 1757

Jacob, son of Jacob Kerty and Maria, b. November 6, 1756, bapt. December 5, 1756. Spon: David Dieterich, Magdalene Bloch, wife of Michael Bloch.
Verena, daughter of Henry Behr and Verena, b. September 16, 1756, bapt. December 19, 1756. Spon: Jacob Behr and Verena Steiner.
Anna Elizabeth, daughter of George Bloch and Anna Elizabeth, b. December 13, 1756, bapt. December 26, 1756. Spon: Henrich Bloecker and wife Louisa.

1757

John, son of Herman Geissel and Anna, b. January 6, 1757, bapt. January 9, 1757. Spon: John Geisel and Anna Tranck.
Peter, son of Peter Zollinger and Barbara, b. December 22, 1756, bapt. January 9, 1757. Spon: Parents.
Henry, son of Jacob Sorber and Anna, b. October 13, 1756, bapt. October 14, 1756, by Mr. Steiner. Spon: Henry Ernst and wife.
Godfried, son of Godfried Bockius and Philippina Catharine, b. December 26, 1756, bapt. January 9, 1757. Spon: Parents.
Elizabeth, daughter of Sirach Schudy and Barbara, b. September 26, 1756, bapt. January 23, 1757. Spon: Jacob Zebly and Elizabeth.
John George, son of John Bockius and Elizabeth, b. January 29, 1757, bapt. February 20, 1757. Spon: Parents.
Joanna Elizabeth, daughter of John Peter Tranck and Mary Magdalene, b. February 28, 1757, bapt. March 6, 1757. Spon: Joanna Elizabeth Tranck.
Anna Margaret, daughter of Peter Bockius and Maria, b. February 8, 1757, bapt. March 20, 1757. Spon: Parents.
Susanna, daughter of John Gaertner and Eva Catharine, b. September 3, 1753, bapt. March 21, 1757. Spon: Christian Gress and wife Susanna.
Susanna, daughter of Sebastian Mueller and Barbara, b. December 7, 1755, bapt. March 21, 1757. Spon: The father.
Joseph, son of Sebastian Mueller and Barbara, b. January 18, 1757, bapt. March 21, 1757. Spon: The father.
Anna Eva, daughter of John Gaertner and Eva Catharine, b. January 18, 1757, bapt. March 21, 1757. Spon: The mother.
Rachel, daughter of Michael Conrad and Elizabeth, b. November 14, 1756, bapt. April 11, 1757. Spon: Jacob Conrad and wife Rachel.

Barbara, daughter of Adam Farner and Sarah, b. April 10, 1757, bapt. April 11, 1757. Spon: Michael Smith and wife Barbara.
Jacob, son of Henry Ernst and Susanna, b. April 16, 1754, bapt. April 11, 1757. Spon: Jacob Sorber and wife Anna.
Susanna, daughter of Henry Ernst and Susanna, b. January 22, 1756, bapt. April 11, 1757. Spon: Parents.
Dorothea, daughter of Melchior Meng and Maria, b. ----, bapt. April 11, 1757. Spon: Dorothea Meng.
Jacob, son of Melchior Meng and Maria, b. April 1, 1756, bapt. April 11, 1757. Spon: The father.
John Nicholas, son of William Heintz and Juliana Catharine, b. April 19, 1757, bapt. May 1, 1757. Spon: John Nicholas Schreiner.
Anna Barbara, daughter of John Stricker and Anna, b. March 28, 1757, bapt. May 1, 1757. Spon: Theobald Diehl and wife Magdalene.
John, son of Jacob Kibler and Mary Magdalene, b. April 19, 1757, bapt. May 1, 1757. Spon: John Kibler and Anna Kibler.
Catharine, daughter of Peter Pfeiffer and Anna Margaret, b. December 4, 1756, bapt. May 15, 1757. Spon: John Lehr and Catharine Kolb, single.
John, son of John Bürgerhof and Anna, b. March 8, 1756, bapt. May 15, 1757. Spon: John Burgerhof and wife Anna Catharine.
John, son of John Benner and Elizabeth, b. May 10, 1757, bapt. May 30, 1757. Spon: John Mueller and wife Margaret.
Jacob, son of John George Benner and Magdalene, b. May 8, 1757, bapt. May 30, 1757. Spon: Jacob Widman and wife Susanna.
John Adam, son of Henry Huesler and Anna, b. May 16, 1757, bapt. May 30, 1757. Spon: Adam Lotz and Maria Ruchtin, single.
John, son of Andrew Gemmel and Regina, b. January 6, 1757, bapt. May 30, 1757. Spon: Parents.
John Henry, son of John Adam Schneider and Anna Catharine, b. April 11, 1757, bapt. June 19, 1757. Spon: Parents.
John Rudolph, son of Leonard Froelich and Catharine, b. ----, bapt. June 19, 1757. Spon: Rudolph Maurer and wife Anna.
John Casper, son of Robert Wilson, servant at Casper Geyer's, b. ----, bapt. June 20, 1757. Spon: Casper Geyer and wife Elizabeth.
John Gerhard, son of Henry Weidner and Catharine Elizabeth, b. ---, bapt. August 7, 1757. Spon: Gerhard Huhn and wife Maria.
Anna Maria, daughter of Casper Sorber and Barbara, b. August 16, 1757, bapt. August 21, 1757. Spon: Rudolph Sorber and wife Anna Maria.
Daniel, son of Gerhard Bornhuetter and Catharine, b. June 12, 1757, bapt. August 21, 1757. Spon: Daniel Huhn and wife Augustina.
Henry, son of John van der Lind and Catharine, b. March 20, 1757, bapt. August 28, 1757. Spon: Henry Stoffel and wife Eva.
Albrecht, son of Abraham Hauser and Christine, b. August 17, 1757, bapt. September 11, 1757. Spon: Albrecht Hackenmueller.
John Adam, son of John Seibold and Elizabeth, b. September 3, 1757, bapt. September 11, 1757. Spon: Adam Schiesler.
Elizabeth, daughter of Andrew Weckgaesser and Susanna, b. January 16, 1757, bapt. September 29, 1757. Spon: William Stoy (pastor) and wife Elizabeth.
Jacob, son of Conrad Mog and Elizabeth, b. August 10, 1757, bapt.

October 2, 1757. Spon: Jacob Mog and wife Anna.

Peter, son of Rudolph Guettinger and Anna, b. November 28, 1757, bapt. December 10, 1757. Spon: Peter Straub and Catharine Armin, single.

Baptisms by the Rev. John George Alsentz, 1758 - 1767

1758

John Philip, son of John George Mueller and Gertrude, b. November 28, 1757, bapt. January 1, 1758. Spon: John Philip Koerner and wife Catharine.

Magdalene, daughter of Henry Koch and Margaret, b. November 19, 1757, bapt. January 1, 1758. Spon: Peter Dippel and wife Magdalene.

Elizabeth, daughter of Henry Riehr and Nelli Anna, b. December 11, 1757, bapt. January 22, 1758. Spon: Leonard Froelich and wife Elizabeth.

John Peter, son of Simon Dreisbach and Dorothea, b. November 3, 1757, bapt. January 22, 1758. Spon: Peter Thoes and Elizabeth Reinhard, single.

Maria Barbara, daughter of Daniel Huhn and Christine, b. December 26, 1757, bapt. February 19, 1758. Spon: George Fettermann and Maria Barbara Karbach, single.

Henry, son of Henry Leschir and Margaret, b. July 17, 1757, bapt. February 25, 1758. Spon: The father, Luth.

Elizabeth, daughter of Jacob Weidmann and Susanna, b. January 25, 1758, bapt. March 5, 1758. Spon: John George Ries and Elizabeth, grandparents.

Anna Barbara, daughter of Jacob Sorber and Anna, b. ----, bapt. March 12, 1758. Spon: Elizabeth Froely daughter of Henry Froely.

Tobias Adam, son of Peter Meyer and Judith, b. February 24, 1758, bapt. March 19, 1758. Spon: Tobias Adam Koenig and wife.

John, son of Jacob Rebold and wife, b. March 19, 1758, bapt. March 26, 1758. Spon: John Duless' son.

John Christian, son of Andrew Hauberger and Catharine, b. December 17, 1757, bapt. March 26, 1758. Spon: John Christian Kehrbach and Anna Kuntz.

Daniel, son of Jacob Ulm and Mary Magdalene, b. August 22, 1757, bapt. March 27, 1758. Spon: Daniel Jost, single.

Henry, son of George Conrad and Barbara, b. December 24, 1757, bapt. March 27, 1758. Spon: Henry Conrad and wife Magdalene.

John, son of George Edelman and Anna, b. November 17, 1753, bapt. March 27, 1758. Spon: Parents.

Regina, daughter of same parents, b. October 12, 1757, bapt. March 27, 1758. Spon: Parents.

Maria, daughter of John Engel and Anna, b. December 16, 1757, bapt. April 2, 1758. Spon: Parents.

Catharine Sophia, daughter of Christopher Scheibeler and wife, b. February 27, 1758, bapt. April 3, 1758. Spon: George Bender and wife.

John Peter, son of Henry Blecker and Barbara Christine, b. March 27, 1758, bapt. April 9, 1758. Spon: John Peter Dippel and wife Mary Magdalene.

John Charles, son of Charles Arnd and wife, b. March 20, 1758, bapt. April 9, 1758. Spon: John Charles Hay and wife.

Conrad, son of Jacob Friess and Anna Margaret, b. March 31, 1758, bapt. April 23, 758. Spon: Conrad Bohner and wife Christine.
Regina, daughter of Daniel Hill and Elizabeth, b. ----, bapt. April 23, 1758. Spon: Rudolph Schuetz and wife Regina.
Margaret, daughter of John George Strunck and Dorothy, b. ----, bapt. April 23, 1758. Spon: Parents.
Susanna, daughter of Michael Theiss and Barbara, b. August 6, 1757, bapt. May 7, 1758. Spon: Parents.
Catharine, daughter of George Jacob Horden and Magdalene, b. May 9, 1758, bapt. May 21, 1758. Spon: George Nicholas Unruh and Catharine Franck.
Margaret, daughter of Frederick Doll and Elizabeth, b. April 24, 1758, bapt. April 30, 1758. Spon: Parents.
Henry, son of Ludwig Gueting and Elizabeth, b. February 28, 1758, bapt. May 28, 1758. Spon: Henry Funck and wife.
Rudolph, son of Conrad Guentzel and wife Anna, b. January 1, 1756, bapt. May 4, 1758. Spon: Rudolph Goettinger and wife Barbara.
Nicholas, son of Adam Corell and Elizabeth, b. July 31, 1757, bapt. April 30, 1758. Spon: Nicholas Korndoerfer.
Maria Sarah, daughter of Adam Corell and Elizabeth, b. October 24, 1755, bapt. April 30, 1758. Spon: Maria ----.
Anna Barbara, daughter of John Kohler and Maria Agatha, b. May 9, 1758, bapt. May 9, 1758. Spon: John Martin and wife Anna Barbara.
Elizabeth Barbara, daughter of Jacob Drein and Rosina, b. May 3, 1758, bapt. May 28, 1758. Spon: Bernard Brand and wife Eva Barbara.
Mary Magdalene, daughter of Frederick Hitzebeck and Catharine, b. March 3, 1758, bapt. May 28, 1758. Spon: John Zumbro and Mary Magdalene Schick, single.
Philip William and Elias, sons of Conrad Schuetz and Catharine, b. January 31, 1758, bapt. June 2, 1758. Spon: Philip William Otterbein, pastor in Lancaster and Jacob Hegi and Maria.
Willia, son of Jacob Hegi and Maria, b. January 21, 1758, bapt. June 2, 1758. Spon: Conrad Schuetz and wife Catharine.
John, son of Jacob Schmid and Maria Eva, b. November 17, 1757, bapt. June 25, 1758. Spon: Parents.
John Joseph, son of Adam Schaefer and Anna Catharine, b. May 24, bapt. June 25, 1758. Spon: Parents.
Anna Maria, daughter of Conrad Rivert and Eva, b. February 16, 1757, bapt. July 16, 1758. Spon: Jacob ---- and wife Anna Maria.
Elizabeth, daughter of Anthony Braun and Elizabeth, b. June 23, 1758, bapt. June 28, 1758. Spon: Christine Rick.
Peter, son of John Albrecht Hesseler and Eva Elizabeth, b. June 12, 1758, bapt. June 28, 1758. Spon: grandmother.
Adam Lutz's wife Barbara nee Levering, Mennonites, of ----, b. 1725, bapt. August 6, 1758. Spon: ----.
Maria Elizabeth, daughter of Frederick Roemer and Anna Christine, b. April 15, 1758, bapt. August 13, 1758. Spon: Henry Schuetz and wife Maria Elizabeth.
John, son of Valentine Rost and Catharine, b. March 4, 1758, bapt. August 13, 1758. Spon: Parents.
Abraham and Isaac, sons of Abraham Bettillion and Margaret, b. August 14, 1758, bapt. August 19, 1758. Spon: Theobald Thiel

and wife and Casper Geyer and wife.

John Nicholas, son of John Nicholas Keisel and Anna Eva, b. July 9, 1758, bapt. August 20, 1758. Spon: John Nicholas Singer and wife.

Anna Elizabeth, daughter of Leonard Kesseler and Elizabeth, b. July 18, 1758, bapt. August 20, 1758. Spon: Henry Cramer and wife.

Elizabeth, daughter of Philip Dotter and Jannike, b. July 19, 1758, bapt. August 20, 1758. Spon: Elizabeth Dotter, single sister of the father, in Whitpain.

George, son of Charles Widerhold and Susanna, b. July 11, 1758, bapt. August 13, 1758. Spon: George Alsentz, p.t. pastor here.

John Ernest, son of John Jacob Riess and Christine Dorothea, born August 15, 1758, bapt. August 27, 1758. Spon: John Ernest Junken.

Elizabeth, daughter of Adam Schneider and Anna Catharine, b. July 7, 1758, bapt. August 27, 1758. Spon: Parents.

John, son of Peter Lehmann and Maria, b. July 13, 1758, bapt. September 3, 1758. Spon: Isaac Burbon and wife.

Anna Maria, daughter of Henry Schreveler and Anna Maria, b. July 25, 1758, bapt. September 10, 1758. Spon: Christopher Scheibeler and wife.

John, son of Henry Baehr and Veronica, b. July 19, 1758, bapt. September 10, 1758. Spon: Parents.

Elizabeth, daughter of Samuel Basserman and Judith, b. September 21, 1758, bapt. October 1, 1758. Spon: John Bender and wife Elizabeth.

Elizabeth, daughter of Martin Lorch and Barbara, b. September 1, 1758, bapt. September 24, 1758. Spon: Henry Conrad and wife.

Mary Magdalene, daughter of George Bloch and Anna Elizabeth, b. September 1, 1758, bapt. October 8, 1758. Spon: Michael Bloch and wife Mary Magdalene.

Elizabeth, daughter of John Wigeler and Veronica, b. August 18, 1758, bapt. October 8, 1758. Spon: Michael Cunrad and wife Elizabeth.

Susan Louise, daughter of Herman Duppel (Dippel) and Catharine, b. September 24, 1758, bapt. October 15, 1758. Spon: Martin Kraeuter and wife Susan Louise.

Elizabeth, daughter Anthony Braun and Elizabeth, b. June 23, 1758, bapt. ----. Spon: Spon: Christine Rick.

John Peter, son of John Albrecht Hisseler and Elizabeth, b. June 12, 1758, bapt. ----. Spon: Parents.

Margaret, daughter of Jacob Nerach and Anna, b. October 29, 1758, bapt. December 3, 1758. Spon: Henry Koch and wife Margaret.

Leonard, son of Henry Summer, dec. and Veronica, b. April 27, 1758, bapt. November 12, 1758. Spon: Leonard Froelich.

John Philip, son of Henry Wunderlich and Maria Elizabeth, b. November 27, 1758, bapt. December 10, 1758. Spon: John Philip Achenbach.

Peter, son of ----, b. ----, bapt. December 3, 1758. Spon: Peter Steeg and Miss Reinhard.

Mary Magdalene, daughter of Jacob Scheig and Anna Magdalene, b. November 2, 1758, bapt. December 17, 1758. Spon: George Delcker and wife Maria Agatha.

John, son of Herman Ohrner and Anna Margaret, b. November 24, 1758, bapt. December 17, 1758. Spon: John Bergenhoff and wife Anna Cath., grandparents.

John Jacob, son of Herman Ohrner and Anna Margaret, b. November 14, 1756, bapt. December 17, 1758. Spon: John Jacob Huth and wife.

David, son of Ulrich Merke and Veronica, b. November 8, 1758, bapt. December 25, 1758. Spon: David Ankerbiler and Anna Mayer, single.

Jonathan, son of Jonathan Klimpen, dec. and Anna Gertrude, b. October 24, 1758, bapt. December 25, 1758. Spon: Jacob Coleman and wife Eva Maria.

1759

John George, son of George Brunner and Margaret, b. October 29, 1758, bapt. January 18, 1759. Spon: John Grop and wife.

Jacob, son of Jacob Handsche and Elizabeth, b. January 10, 1759, bapt. January 18, 1759. Spon: John Grider and wife Elizabeth.

Daniel, son of Daniel Schattele and Anna, b. February 29, 1758 and bapt. January 18, 1759. Spon: John Grider and wife Elizabeth.

Catharine, daughter of Henry Buse and Catharine, b. May 29, 1758, bapt. January 18, 1759. Spon: Parents.

Elizabeth, daughter Martin Laetty and Elizabeth, b. August 26, 1758, bapt. January 18, 1759. Spon: Parents.

Barbara, daughter of Sirach Schudy and Barbara, b. December 25, 1758, bapt. January 18, 1759. Spon: Parents.

Maria, daughter of Francis L'angloise and Elizabeth, b. April 30, 1757, bapt. January 18, 1759. Spon: Parents.

Anna Maria, daughter of Lawrence Schmidt and Helena, b. October 7, 1758, bapt. January 24, 1759. Spon: Adam Haas and wife Anna Maria.

Jacob, son of Frederick Meile and Barbara, b. January 10, 1759, bapt. January 21, 1759. Spon: Jacob Maurer, single.

Peter, son of Leonard Froely and Catharine, b. January 23, 1759, bapt. January 28, 1759. Spon: Peter Brendly and wife Apollonia.

Anna Maria, daughter of Daniel Huhn and Christine, b. January 26, 1759, bapt. February 11, 1759. Spon: Gerard Huhn and wife Anna Maria.

Daniel, son of John Kerbach and Sybil, b. December 5, 1758, bapt. February 11, 1759. Spon: Daniel Huhn and wife Christine.

Anna Maria, daughter of John George Bickes and Anna Barbara, b. January 10, 1759, bapt. February 18, 1759. Spon: Michael Steitz and wife Anna Maria.

Andrew, son of Martin Heidler and Elizabeth Joanna, b. February 4, 1759, bapt. February 18, 1759. Spon: Andrew Wackerberg.

Henry, son of Rudolph Weiss and Anna, b. December 18, 1758, February 1, 1758 [probably intended 1759]. Spon: Henry Baehr and wife Veronica.

Elizabeth, daughter of Gerard Bornhetter Elizabeth Catharine, b. December 1, 1758, bapt. February 25, 1759. Spon: Anthony Huhn and wife Elizabeth.

Veronica, daughter of Peter Zollinger and Barbara, b. November 23, 1758, bapt. March 4, 1759. Spon: Ulrich Zollinger and wife Veronica.

Elizabeth, daughter of Jacob Koebeler and Magdalene, b. January 5, 1759, bapt. March 4, 1759. Spon: John Grider and wife

Elizabeth.

John Casper, son of John Casper Schlatter and Barbara, b. March 22, 1759, bapt. April 8, 1759. Spon: Henry Merke and wife Margaret.

Anna Catharine, daughter of John George Reichwein and Susanna, b. March 4, 1759, bapt. April 8, 1759. Spon: Andrew Heiberger and Anna Catharine.

Jacob, son of Matthew Sailer and Anna Maria, b. March 26, 1759, bapt. April 22, 1759. Spon: Jacob Sailer and wife Margaret.

John Frederick, son of Godfried Wilken and Christine, b. February 2, 1759, bapt. April 22, 1759. Spon: John Frederick Delinger and wife Catharine.

Philip, son of John Bokius and Elizabeth, b. March 19, 1759, bapt. April 22, 1759. Spon: Parents.

Anna Maria, daughter of Peter Pfeiffer and Anna Maria, b. February 9, 1759, bapt. April 22, 1759. Spon: John George Brooss and wife Anna Margaret.

John Frederick, son of Jost Weil and Catharine, b. December 25, 1758, bapt. April 22, 1759. Spon: Frederick Schmid and Anna Marie Kab.

John George, son of John Geo. Braunsberg and Anna, b. January 17, 1759, bapt. April 22, 1759. Spon: Parents.

John Leonard, son of Henry Miller and Anna Maria, b. October 16, bapt. April 23, 1759. Spon: Parents.

Susanna, daughter of Melchior Meng and Maria, b. April 7, 1759, bapt. April 29, 1759. Spon: Parents.

Elizabeth, daughter of Henry Funck and Christine, b. November --, 1758, bapt. April 22, 1759. Spon: Jacob Bertsch and Elizabeth.

A mulatto, Aaron, child of an unknown negro and Joanna Wilhelm, a white woman, b. ----, bapt. May 7, 1759. Spon: George Klinger.

Conrad, son of George Volkmar and Anna, b. December 29, 1758, bapt. May 6, 1759. Spon: Conrad Kerlinger.

Anna Margaret, daughter of John Henry Grimm and Apollonia, b. July 20, 1758, bapt. May 14, 1759. Spon: Anna Margaret Kilgerum, grandmother.

John, son of Jacob Coleman and Eva Maria, b. March --, 1759, bapt. May 24, 1759. Spon: Lawrence Ries and wife Anna Cornelia.

Anna Margaret, daughter of Jacob Daenig and Anna Maria, b. May 26, 1759, bapt. May 31, 1759. Spon: Anna Margaret Daenig.

Jacob, son of Jacob Bleker and Susanna, b. April 20, 1759, bapt. June 3, 1759. Spon: Parents.

John, son of Henry Meyer and Margaret, b. January 2, 1759, bapt. June 3, 1759. Spon: B. Baumward and wife Eva.

John Peter, son of Christian Ritz and Juliana, b. May 22, 1759, bapt. June 3, 1759. Spon: John Peter Paris and wife Magdalene.

David, son of Philip Engert and Catharine, b. April 16, 1759, bapt. June 4, 1759. Spon: Henry Rummen, single.

Frederick, son of Henry Cunrad and Magdalene, b. April 29, 1759, bapt. June 4, 1759. Spon: Frederick Doll and wife Anna Elizabeth.

Maria Barbara, daughter of Jacob Anderson and Maria, b. March 30, 1759, bapt. June 4, 1759. Spon: George Cunrad and wife Maria Barbara.

Jacob, son of Rudolph Maurer and Anna, b. September 29, 1758, bapt. June 10, 1759. Spon: Jacob Maurer and ----.

Magdalene, daughter of Valentine Hiss and Christine, b. June 3, 1759, bapt. June 10, 1759. Spon: Jacob Horder and wife Magdalene.
Maria Catharine, daughter of Godfried Bokius and Philippina, b. June 18, 1759, bapt. July 1, 1759. Spon: Maria Catharine Rein, grandmother.
Conrad, son of Conrad Schabecker and Agnesia (Agnes), b. May 8, 1759, bapt. August 12, 1759. Spon: Jacob Gaensel and wife Catharine.
Peter, son of Jon Nicholas Saenger and Anna Margaret, b. July 12, 1759, bapt. August 26, 1759. Spon: Peter Lohnes, single.
Jacob, son of Jacob Sorber and Anna, b. September 14, 1759, bapt. September 16, 1759. Spon: Parents.
Elizabeth, daughter of Nicholas Hausecker and Catharine Elizabeth, b. October 1, 1759, bapt. October 14, 1759. Spon: Elizabeth Kress and Andrew Greiner, single.
Valentine, son of Jacob Schmid and Maria Eva, b. April 10, 1759, bapt. October 31, 1759. Spon: Valentine Petri and wife, and grandparents.
Anna Margaret, daughter of David Reinhard and Anna Margaret, b. June 31, 1759, bapt. October 21, 1759. Spon: Elizabeth Jost, of Whitpain.
Anna Maria, daughter of John Conrad Skiger and Catharine, b. February 14, 1759, bapt. November 10, 1759. Spon: Anna Maria Ley, single.
John George, son of John George Bender and Magdalene, b. November 7, 1759, bapt. November 25, 1759. Spon: Parents.
John Philip, son of Nicholas Korndoerfer and Maria Margaret, b. November 24, 1759, bapt. December 6, 1759. Spon: John Philip Dotterer and wife Janniken.
Maria Dorothea, daughter of Henry Buse and Catharine, b. October -, 1759, bapt. November 25, 1759. Spon: Jacob Zubely and Maria Dorothea Basler.
Catharine Verena, daughter of John Heisch and Catharine, b. June 27, 1759, bapt. December 2, 1759. Spon: Conrad Kemp and wife Verena.
Anna Elizabeth, daughter of Frederick Doll and Elizabeth, b. December 14, 1759, bapt. December 26, 1759. Spon: Parents.

1760
Margaret, daughter of John Engel and Anna, b. August 21, 1759, bapt. January 27, 1760. Spon: Parents.
Henry, son of John Bender and Elizabeth, b. January 13, 1760, bapt. February 3, 1760. Spon: Parents.
Jacob, son of Rudolph Lang and Sophia, b. December 25, 1759, bapt. February 6, 1760. Spon: Jacob Mayer and wife Anna.
A child of Jacob Handsche and Elizabeth, b. ----, bapt. February 6, 1760. Spon: ----.
Joseph, son of ---- Rohny and wife, b. November 19, 1759, bapt. February 6, 1760. Spon: Henry Brunner and wife Barbara.
Elizabeth, daughter of Philip Wentz and Apollonia, b. December 27, 1759, bapt. February 22, 1760. Spon: Parents.
Daniel, son of Philip Sperr and wife, b. February 3, 1760, bapt. February 22, 1760. Spon: Daniel Joost.
Mary Magdalene, daughter of Jacob Gress and Mary Magdalene, b.

October 5, 1759, bapt. February 22, 1760. Spon: Lawrence Enters and Mary Magdalene Schick.

Lawrence, son of Michael Steitz and Anna Maria, b. February 8, 1760, bapt. February 24, 1760. Spon: Lawrence Bast and wife, grandparents.

Anna Barbara, daughter of of Charles Arnd and Anna, b. February 15, 1760, bapt. March 2, 1760. Spon: John George Bickes and wife Anna Barbara.

Margaret, daughter of Abraham Bettillion and Margaret, b. February 24, 1760, bapt. March 16, 1760. Spon: Theobald Diel and wife Mary Magdalene.

Anna Barbara, daughter of Lawrence Herschinger and Anna Barbara, b. January 3, 1754, bapt. April 6, 1760. Spon: Charles Arnd and wife Anna.

John Christopher, son of same parents, b. March 23, 1758, bapt. April 6, 1760. Spon: Christopher Nutz and wife Maria Anna.

Susanna Barbara, daughter of Lawrence Herschinger and Anna Barbara, b. January 14, 1756, bapt. April 6, 1760. Spon: Jacob Wasser and wife Anna Barbara.

Henry, son of Jacob Wasser and Anna Barbara, b. March 17, 1760, bapt. April 6, 1760. Spon: Conrad Kunkely and wife Barbara.

Lawrence, son of Jacob Ries and Christine Dorothy, b. March --, 1760, bapt. March 30, 1760. Spon: Lawrence Ries and wife Cornelia.

A son of Adam Schneider and Joanna Catharine, b. March 1, 1760, bapt. April 27, 1760. Spon: Gerard Huhn and wife Anna Maria.

Anna Elizabeth, daughter of Abraham Henrich and Elizabeth, b. February 8, 1760, bapt. May 11, 1760. Spon: Michael Bloch and wife Mary Magdalene.

Dorothea, daughter of Jacob Biöt and Margaret, b. March 31, 1760, bapt. May 18, 1760. Spon: Dorothea ----.

Anna, daughter of Conrad Kramer and Anna, b. April 1, 1760, bapt. May 18, 1760. Spon: Samuel Neuschwanger and wife Adelheid.

Samuel, son of Samuel Neuschwanger and Adelheyd, b. September 14, 1758, bapt. May 18, 1760. Spon: Conrad Kramer and wife Anna.

Anna Catharine, daughter of Conrad Dinges and Elizabeth, b. March 6, 1760, bapt. May 25, 1760. Spon: Philip Koerner and wife Anna Catharine.

Rudolph, son of Henry Baehr and Verena, b. March 30, 1760, bapt. May 25, 1760. Spon: Rudolph Weiss and wife Anna.

John, son of Peter Schmid and Maria Elizabeth, b. May 29, 1760, bapt. June 15, 1760. Spon: John Bender and wife Elizabeth.

Elizabeth, daughter of Peter Zollinger and Barbara, b. May 24, 1760, bapt. June 27, 1760. Spon: Parents.

Philip, son of Philip Rittershan and Martha, b. May 16, 1760, bapt. June 29, 1760. Spon: Philip Dotterer and Jannetta, his wife.

Maria Catharine, daughter of Peter Bock and Mary Magdalene, b. May 11, 1760, bapt. June 29, 1760. Spon: Jacob Schuetz and Veronica

Daniel, son of Jacob Hegy and Maria, b. March 28, 1760, bapt. June 27, 1760. Spon: Parents.

John, son of Jacob Schuetz and Veronica, b. May 7, 1760, bapt. June 1, 1760 at Whitpain. Spon: John Eberd and wife, grandparents.

Anna Eva, daughter of Nicholas Knisel and Anna Eva, b. January 4, 1760, bapt. June 1, 1760. Spon: George Kunrath and Maria

Barbara.
A daughter of Rudolph Buegy and wife, b. ----, bapt. July 14, 1760. Spon: Parents.
A son of Jacob Schuster and wife, b. ----, bapt. July 14, 1760. Spon: Parents.
Philip, son of Adam Lotz and Barbara, b. June 19, 1760, bapt. July 4, 1760. Spon: Philip Dotterer and wife Jannetta.
John Henry, son of John Graff and Elizabeth, b. December 7, 1758, bapt. July 4, 1760. Spon: Francis Graff.
Maria Elizabeth, daughter of same parents, b. April 5, 1760, bapt. July 4, 1760. Spon: Parents.
John Hartman, son of Jacob Rebold and wife, b. July 14, 1760, bapt. July 20, 1760. Spon: John Hartman Adam and wife, grandparents.
John Jacob, son of David Ungerbiler and Anna, b. August 17, 1760, bapt. September 21, 1760. Spon: Jacob Mayer and Anna Barbara Kuebeler.
George Philip, son of Andrew Vey and Sophia, b. August 1, 1760, bapt. September 21, 1760. Spon: George Philip Fritschi and wife Catharine.
Jacob, son of Jacob Schumacher and Judith, b. September 19, 1760, bapt. October 9, 1760. Spon: Jacob Kuhn and wife Susanna.
Robert, son of Daniel Helffenstein and Sarah, b. July 24, 1760, bapt. October 22, 1760. Spon: Henry Ernst and wife.
Elizabeth, daughter of Nicholas Helffenstein and Rachel, b. May 17, 1760, bapt. October 22, 1760. Spon: Eva Eliz. Helffenstein, grandmother.
Anna, daughter of Henry Isler and Anna, b. April 6, 1760, bapt. October 26, 1760. Spon: Jacob Herman and Anna Herman.
Maria Elizabeth, daughter of Conrad Schuetz and Catharine, b. August 19, 1760, bapt. October 24, 1760. Spon: Gerard Henry Schuetz and wife Maria Elizabeth.
Philip, son of Philip Krigbaum and Maria Elizabeth, b. September 26, 1759, bapt. October 24, 1760. Spon: Conrad Schuetz and wife Catharine.
John Christian, son of Daniel Huhn and Christine, b. October 15, 1760, bapt. November 9, 1760. Spon: John Christian Kerbach and wife.
Anna Maria, daughter of Jacob Brown and Maria Magdalena, b. September 22, 1760, bapt. November 9, 1760. Spon: Philip Fuchs and wife Anna Catharine.
John Henry, son of John Henry Grimm and Maria Apollonia, b. August 25, 1760, bapt. November 15, 1760. Spon: Parents.
Abraham, son of Philip Dotterer and Jeanette, b. October 25, 1760, bapt. November 16, 1760. Spon: Abraham Paul and wife Beeltge.
Esther and Anna Maria, daughters of Jacob Fisler and Barbara, b. September 29, 1757, b. November 17, 1760. Spon: Parents.
Susanna, daughter of Jacob Fisler and Barbara, b. September 29, 1758. Spon: Parents.
Frederick, son of Frederick Hiltzebeck and Catharine, b. September 24, 1760, bapt. November 17, 1760. Spon: Parents.
John, son of Peter Bokius and Maria, b. September 11, 1759, bapt. August 1, 1760. Spon: Parents.
Anna Catharine, daughter of John Sorber and Anna, b. August 27, 1760, bapt. December 14, 1760. Spon: Parents.
Maria Susanna, daughter of George Kunrath and Maria Barbara, b.

December 10, 1760, bapt. December 26, 1760 in Witpen. Spon: --.
John, son of Jacob Kuebeler and Magdalene, b. October 20, 1760, bapt. December 25, 1760. Spon: John Kuebeler and Anna, grandparents.
Catharine Apollonia, daughter of Christian Lentz and wife, b. November 16, 1760, bapt. December 26, 1760. Spon: H. Mitchel and wife.
Daniel, son of Valentine Klages and Elizabeth, b. August 11, 1760, bapt. December 25, 1760. Spon: Daniel Kümpman (Kampman), single.
Henry, son of William Dosten and Eliabeth, b. August 7, 1760, bapt. August 21, 1760. Spon: Henry Froely and wife.

1761
Margaret, daughter of Henry Ernst, dec. and Susanna, b. December 23, 1760, bapt. January 19, 1761. Spon: Eva Elizabeth Helffenstein, grandmother.
Henry, son of Anthony Huhn and Elizabeth, b. December 5, 1760, bapt. January 25, 1761. Spon: Henry Hoffman and wife Susanna, grandparents.
Daniel, son of Melchior Meng and Maria, b. Septmeber 16, 1760, bapt. January 25, 1761. Spon: Christopher Meng and wife Catharine, grandparents.
John Godfried, son of Charles Widerhold and Susanna, b. ----, bapt. January 18, 1761. Spon: John Godfried Thiel and wife.
Anna Catharine, daughter of Anthony Brown and Elizabeth, b. October 13, 1760, bapt. February 3, 1761. Spon: Parents.
A daughter of Christian Jauch and Mary Magdalene, b. January 4, 1761, bapt. February 25, 1761. Spon: Parents.
George William, son of William Spira and Maria, b. February 25, 1760, bapt. February 22, 1761. Spon: George Michael Kraft and Martha Meyer, single.
Rudolph, son of Rudolph Weiss and Anna, b. December 25, 1760, bapt. March 1, 1761. Spon: Rudolph Schuetz and wife Rachel.
George Michael, son of Peter Lang and Anna Margaret, b. September 22, 1760, bapt. March 15, 1761. Spon: George Michael Lang in his name: Geo. Casper Heft.
John George and Elizabeth, son and daughter of Jacob Schmid and Maria Eva, b. March 4, 1761, bapt. March 15, 1761. Spon: John Geo. Gerster and Eva Frederick Hass and wife Elizabeth.
A daughter of Nicholas Rehbein and Sophia, b. January 1, 1761, bapt. March 15, 1761. Spon: Parents.
Maria Albertina, daughter of John Dauenheim and Maria Magdalena, b. January 17, 1761, bapt. March 22, 1761. Spon: John Gerlach and wife Maria Albertina.
Ludwig (Lewis), son of Peter Weissman and Elizabeth Margaret, b. February 20, 1761, bapt. March 22, 1761. Spon: Ludwig Bernhard and wife.
Anna, daughter of Henry Mayer and Margaret, b. August 30, 1760, bapt. March 22, 1761. Spon: Henry Oberlander and wife Verena.
Anna Maria, daughter of Michael Banword and Eva, b. March 25, 1760, bapt. March 22, 1761. Spon: Henry Mayer and Magdaene Klein.
Andrew, son of Michael Theiss and Barbara, b. April 1, 1760, bapt. March 29, 1761. Spon: Parents.
Susanna, daughter of John George Schettinger and Joanna Wilhelmina,

b. January 9, 1761, bapt. March 29, 1761. Spon: John George Gass and wife Susanna.

Anna Catharine, daughter of Jacob Fries and Margaret, b. December 29, 1760, bapt. March 22, 1761. Spon: Elias Nestler and wife Anna Catharine.

Elizabeth Joost, nee Scherrin, daughter of ----, aged 27 years, bapt. April 5, 1761. Spon: ----.

Philip Saenger, son of ----, aged 22 years, bapt. April 5, 1761. Spon: ----.

Jacob, son of Daniel Joost and Elizabeth, b. December 7, 1760, bapt. April 5, 1761. Spon: Jacob Joost and wife Elizabeth, grandparents.

Jacob, son of Casper Schlatter and Barbara, b. March 5, 1761, bapt. April 5, 1761. Spon: Jacob Gubler and wife Maria Elizabeth.

Frederick, son of Frederick Kern and Anna Maria, b. March 22, 1761, bapt. April 5, 1761. Spon: Parents.

John Peter, son of Felix Fenner and Maria Eva, b. March 23, 1761, bapt. April 5, 1761. Spon: John Peter Dick, single, from Whitpain.

Maria Magdalena, daughter of Abraham Hauser and Christine, b. April 1, 1761, bapt. May 3, 1761. Spon: Henry Rumman and Maria Magdalena Kern, single.

Elizabeth Barbara, daughter of George Reichwein and Susanna, b. April 22, 1761, bapt. May 3, 1761. Spon: Jacob Hahn and wife Elizabeth Barbara.

Anna Catharine, daughter of Peter Wolff and Juliana Catharine, b. January 30, 1761, bapt. May 4, 1761. Spon: Parents.

John Jacob, son of John Zumbro and Maria Elizabeth, b. February 22, 1761, bapt. May 19, 1761. Spon: John Jacob Zumbro and wife Margaret, from Whitpain.

Anna Maria, daughter of Rudolph Guttinger and Anna, b. February 13, 1761, bapt. April 26, 1761. Spon: Ulrich Nisle and wife Anna Maria.

Anna Catharine, daughter of Peter Reuss and Barbara, b. January 29, 1761, bapt. May 11, 1761. Spon: Gertrude Delcker.

Anna Maria, daughter of Conrad Brotzman and Anna Cunigunda, b. April 16, 1761, bapt. May 26, 1761. Spon: Valentine Paff and wife Anna Maria.

Elizabeth Weber, wife of Jacob Weber, nee Schneider, aged 27 years, also her children:

John Jacob Neiss, son of Jacob Weber and Elizabeth, Nee Schneider (whose father died), b. March 20, 1755, bapt. May 31, 1761. Spon: ----.

Abraham, son of Elizabeth, nee Schneider (whose father died), b. March 20, 1757, bapt. May 31, 1761. Spon: ----.

Catharine Weber, daughter of Jacob Weber and Elizabeth, nee Schneider (whose father died), b. July 29, 1759, bapt. May 31, 1761. Spon: Parents.

John Adam Blum, son of Christopher Blum and wife, b. February 21, 1761, bapt. May 17, 1761. Spon: John Adam Schihler and wife.

Matthew, son of Andrew Kern and Catharine, b. April --, 1761, bapt. May 31, 1761. Spon: Matthew Kern and wife.

John, son of Michael Conrad and Elizabeth, b. April 4, 1761, bapt. June 14, 1761. Spon: John Widmer.

John Gerlach, son of John Gerlach Bornhuetter and Catharine, b.

April 8, 1761, bapt. July 5, 1761. Spon: John Gerlach Hammer and Maria Juliana Tripler.

John, son of (John *added*) Martin Mayer and Anna Magdalene, b. January 23, 1761, bapt. July 5, 1761. Spon: John Bergenhoffer and wife Anna Catharine.

Elizabeth, daughter of Peter Banno and Elizabeth, b. June 16, 1761, bapt. July 5, 1761. Spon: John George Ries and Anna Elizabeth, grandparents.

John, son of John Engel and Anna, b. February 28, 1761, bapt. August 2, 1761. Spon: Parents.

Jacob, son of Nicholas Rehbein, Jr. and Magdalene, b. April 5, 1761, bapt. August 9, 1761. Spon: Parents.

Esther, daughter of Rudolph Buegy and Anna, b. October 29, 1760, bapt. August 5, 1761. Spon: Parents.

Peter, son of John Bockius and Elizabeth, b. ----, bapt. August 16, 1761. Spon: Parents.

Jacob, son of Matthew Miller and Anna Margaret, b. August 12, 1761, bapt. August 16, 1761. Spon: Jacob Weidman and wife Susanna.

John, son of ---- Risch and wife, b. August 10, 1761, bapt. August 17, 1761. Spon: Parents.

Anna Barbara, daughter of Jacob Sorber and Anna, b. September 13, 1761, bapt. September 26, 1761. Spon: Parents.

Henry, son of Herman Orner and Anna Margaret, b. January 7, 1761, bapt. September 7, 1761, by Mr. Schlatter. Spon: Henry Schuetz and wife.

Anna, daughter of Henry Mayer and Barbara, b. October 10, 1761, bapt. November 18, 1761. Spon: George Eberhard and wife Anna.

1762

Margaret, daughter of Peter Schmid and Maria Elizabeth, b. December 24, 1761, bapt. April 11, 1762 by Mr. Schlatter. Spon: John Mueller and wife Margaret.

Christopher, son of Frederick Haas and Elizabeth, b. January 22, 1762, bapt. March 14, 1761, by Mr. Schlatter, died June 15, 1764. Spon: Christopher Meng and wife Catharine.

Francis, daughter of John Groff and Elizabeth, b. January 15, 1762, bapt. March 14, 1762. Spon: ----.

Joseph, son of Jacob Sorber and Anna, b. October 20, 1762, bapt. October 27, 1762. Spon: Parents.

Anna Barbara, daughter of Henry Isler and Anna, b. October 1, 1761, bapt. October 31, 1762. Spon: Henry Mercky and wife Anna Barbara.

John Peter, son of William Kampman and Maria Catharine, b. February 24, 1762, bapt. October 31, 1762. Spon: John Peter Nayman and wife Margaret, grandparents.

Christine Sophia, daughter of Daniel Kampman and Elizabeth, b. July 28, 1762, bapt. October 31, 1762. Spon: Jacob Maurer and Christine Sophia.

Maria, daughter of Melchior Meng and Maria, b. September 1, 1762, bapt. October 31, 1762. Spon: Parents.

John Jacob, son of Henry Grimm and Apollonia, b. November 5, 1762, bapt. November 7, 1762. Spon: John Jacob Scheich.

Henry, son of Conrad Kuensely and Anna Barbara, b. July 24, 1762, bapt. November 14, 1762. Spon: Henry Summer and Catharine

Froely, single.

Maria Elizabeth, daughter of John Benner and Maria Elizabeth, b. October 9, 1762, bapt. November 14, 1762. Spon: Peter Schmid and wife Maria Elizabeth.

Catharine, daughter of Peter Bockius and Maria, b. March 14, 1762, bapt. November 14, 1762. Spon: Parents.

John, son of Peter Rusch and Elizabeth, b. April 27, 1761, bapt. November 14, 1762. Spon: Parents.

John Jacob, son of Philip Edeborn and Catharine, b. March 24, 1762, bapt. November 14, 1762. Spon: Parents.

Anna Elizabeth, daughter of Christian Jauch and Maria Magdalena, b. September 5, 1762, bapt. November 28, 1762. Spon: Parents.

Martin, son of Philip Wentzel and Maria Christine, b. September 13, 1762, bapt. December 12, 1762. Spon: Martin Schmid and wife Catharine.

Elizabeth, daughter of Michael Schmid and Barbara, b. October 13, 1762, bapt. December 12, 1762. Spon: Parents.

A son of John Stoto and wife, b. ----, bapt. December 12, 1762. Spon: Parents.

Apollonia, daughter of George Unruh and Catharine, b. November 3, 1762, bapt. December 12, 1762. Spon: John Unruh and Apollonia, wife, grandparents.

Joanna, daughter of Jacob Huber and Elizabeth, b. September 15, 1762, bapt. December 12, 1762. Spon: John Wolfeckert and wife Joanna.

1763

Christina Elizabeth, daughter of Henry Oberlander and Veronica, b. November 22, 1762, bapt. January 1, 1763. Spon: John Adam Schissler and wife Anna Margaret.

Maria Sophia, daughter of Christopher Hargischeimer and Sarah Elizabeth, b. December 26, 1762, bapt. January 23, 1763. Spon: Anthony Gilbert and wife Maria Sophia.

John George, son of John George Schottinger and Joanna, b. December 10, 1762, bapt. January 30, 1763. Spon: George Gass and wife Susanna.

Christine, daughter of Andrew Barner and Anna Elizabeth, b. January 14, 1763, bapt. January 30, 1763. Spon: Henry Blecker and wife Christine.

Elizabeth, daughter of Casper Hinckel and Catharine, b. December 13, 1762, bapt. February 3, 1763. Spon: Daniel Kampman and wife Elizabeth.

John, son of Conrad Joost and Regina, b. December 5, 1762, bapt. February 13, 1763. Spon: John Crossman and Maria Does, single.

Eva Maria, daughter of John Ries and Catharine, b. February 16, 1763, bapt. March 13, 1763. Spon: George Kuefer and wife Eva Maria.

Anna Catharine, daughter of Matthew Miller and Anna Margaret, b. Feburary 8, 1763, bapt. March 13, 1763. Spon: Christian Edel and wife Catharine.

John George, son of George Wilky and Anna Maria, b. February 12, 1763, bapt. March 13, 1763. Spon: John George Schuetz and wife Catharine.

John Gerard, son of Daniel Huhn and Christine, b. December 25, 1762, bapt. March 17, 1763. Spon: John Gerhard Huhn and wife

Anna Maria.

Catharine Margaret, daughter of John Kerbach and Sybilla, b. February 1, 1763, bapt. March 17, 1763. Spon: Peter Weckerle and wife Cath. Margaret.

Christine, daughter of Solomon Zell and Sophia, b. March 3, 1763, bapt. April 17, 1763. Spon: Henry Funck and wife Christine.

Maria Margaret, daughter of John Mecklen and Maria Catharine, b. March 2, 1763, bapt. April 25, 1763. Spon: Casper Weiss and wife Maria Margaret.

John George, son of Jacob Schuster and Anna Eva, b. April 5, 1763, bapt. April 25, 1763. Spon: Parents.

Anna Cunigunda, son of Henry Stumpf and Anna Maria, b. March 20, 1763, bapt. May 1, 1763, at Whitpain. Spon: William Clauss and wife Anna Cunigunda.

Fransciscus of John Groff and Elizabeth, b. ----, bapt. May 1, 1763, at Whitpain. Spon: Franciscus Groff, grandfather.

A daughter of George Schaed and Anna Maria, b. April --, 1763, bapt. May 8, 1763. Spon: Parents.

Solomon Zell, son of ----, aged 30 years, bapt. May 8, 1763. Spon: ----.

Henry, son of Henry Schaed and Christine, b. April 24, 1763, bapt. May 15, 1763. Spon: Michael Schoch and wife Margaret.

A daughter of John George Bickes and Barbara, b. April 1, 1763, bapt. May 15, 1763. Spon: Conrad Schuetz and wife Catharine.

Matthias, son of Matthias Heus and Margaret, b. April 5, 1763, bapt. May 15, 1763. Spon: John Gardner and wife Eva Catharine.

Magdalene, daughter of Balthaser Ernst and Anna Maria, b. February 3, 1763, bapt. May 15, 1763. Spon: Parents.

John, son of Samuel Baserman and Judith, b. February 19, 1763, bapt. May 15, 1763. Spon: John Schad and wife.

Jacob, son of Jacob Zuebly and Esther, b. March 30, 1763, bapt. May 15, 1763. Spon: Jacob Naeff and wife Anna.

Jacob, son of Jacob Naeff and Anna, b. March 5, 1763, bapt. May 15, 1763. Spon: Jacob Zuebly and wife Esther.

Martin, son of Martin Luetty and Elizabeth, b. November --, 1762, bapt. May 15, 1763. Spon: Parents.

Anna Maria, daughter of Daniel Joost and Elizabeth, b. September 7, 1762, bapt. May 23, 1763. Spon: Philip Bohm and wife Anna Maria.

Margaret, daughter of Henry Mayer and Margaret, b. August 27, 1762, bapt. May 24, 763. Spon: Henry Oberländer and wife Verena.

Abraham, son of Ulrich Weckerle and Eberhardina, b. April 15, 1763, bapt. June 4, 1763. Spon: Peter Weckerle and wife Catharine Marg.

Anna Maria, daughter of Peter Degen and Catharine, b. March 4, 1763, bapt. June 4, 1763. Spon: Parents.

Elizabeth, daughter of Jacob Gaerdner and Catharine, b. May 7, 1763, bapt. June 12, 1763. Spon: Henry Froely and wife Elizabeth, grandparents.

Jacob, son of Henry Rumman and Dorothy, b. May 26, 1763, bapt. June 26, 1763, in Whitpain. Spon: Jacob Rumman and wife Catharine, grandparents.

A daughter of George Conrad and Maria Barbara, b. July 24, 1763, bapt. August 21, 1763. Spon: ---- Faust and ---- Kniesel.

William, son of Peter Schmid and Maria Elizabeth, b. July 18, 1763, bapt. August 28, 1763. Spon: Parents.

Anna Maria, daughter of Henry Kunrath and Gertrude, b. August 16, 1763, bapt. September 18, 1763. Spon: Henry Stumpf and wife Anna Maria.

John, son of William Clauss and Anna Cunigunda, b. July 17, 1763, bapt. September 18, 1763. Spon: John Marten and wife.

Elizabeth, daughter of John Eberhard and Elizabeth, b. September 7, 1763, bapt. September 18, 1763. Spon: Henry Berky and wife Elizabeth.

Maria Margaret, daughter of Jacob Ache and Maria Eva, b. August 22, 1763, bapt. September 18, 1763. Spon: Herman Ache and wife Maria Paulina.

David, son of Abraham Kehr and Magdalene, b. July 27, 1763, bapt. September 25, 1763. Spon: David Schuvenan and wife Maria, grandparents.

Maria Barbara, daughter of Anthony Huhn and Elizabeth, b. July 28, 1763, bapt. September 25, 1763. Spon: Bernard Guter and Anna Maria Hoffman for Barbara Junk.

Elizabeth, daughter of Jacob Ebrecht and Hannah, b. 1775, bapt. October 2, 1763. Spon: Henry Steltz and wife Margaret.

John Henry, son of Rudolph Ebrecht and Apollonia, b. August 27, 1763, bapt. October 2, 1763. Spon: Henry Steltz and wife Margaret.

Catharine, daughter of Henry Koch and Margaret, b. August 31, 1763, bapt. October 9, 1763. Spon: John Weidmann and Catharine Froely.

John Frederick, son of Frederick Meily and Barbara, b. August 10, 1763, bapt. October 9, 1763. Spon: John Haas and wife Elizabeth.

Maria Magdalena, daughter of Peter Lehman and Maria[*handwritten*] Esther, b. August 17, 1763, bapt. October 9, 1763. Spon: Michael Bloch and wife Maria Magdalene.

Leonard, son of Frederick Altimus and Susanna, b. May 26, 1763, bapt. October 23, 1763. Spon: Leonard Schmid and wife Barbara.

Joseph, son of Jacob Sorber and Anna, b. October 26, 1763, bapt. November 6, 1763. Spon: Joseph Funck and wife Magdalene.

John, son of Henry Mayer and Barbara, b. September 1, 1763, bapt. November 20, 1763. Spon: Casper Sorber and wife.

John, son of Henry Guterman and Charlotte, b. August 30, 1763, bapt. November 20, 1763. Spon: John Lamm, single.

Maria Sophia, daughter of John Roll and Maria Clara, b. June 26, 1763, bapt. December 4, 1763. Spon: John Geisel and wife Maria Sophia.

Margaret, daughter of Charles Wiederhold and Susanna, b. October 25, 1763, bapt. December 4, 1763. Spon: Parents.

1764

Anna, daughter of Jacob Mayer and Barbara, b. December --, 1763, bapt. January 1, 1764. Spon: Jacob Mayer and wife, grandparents.

Anna, daughter of Peter Mayer and Judith, b. October 28, 1763, bapt. January 1, 1764. Spon: Leonard Froely and wife Catharine.

Sarah, daughter of Daniel Haubensack and Juliana, b. January 6,

1764, bapt. February 12, 1764. Spon: Jacob Bauch and wife Rosina.
Catharine, daughter of Christian Gutknecht and Maria Magdelena, b. January 14, 1764, bapt. February 19, 1764. Spon: Kilian Fuehrer and wife Catharine.
Catharine, daughter of Jacob Naglee and Anna, b. January 11, 1764, bapt. February 21, 1764. Spon: Conrad Schuetz and wife Catharine.
Joseph, son of William Dusten and Elizabeth, b. March 1, 1764, bapt. March 11, 1764. Spon: Joseph Funck and wife.
Elizabeth, daughter of Christopher Hargischeimer and Sarah, b. December 16, 1763, bapt. January --, 1764. Spon: Elizabeth Gilbert and George Hargischeimer.
Magdalene, daughter of Peter Ozias and Magdalene, b. January 2, 1764, bapt. March 18, 1764. Spon: Parents.
Catharine, daughter of Michael Theiss and Barbara, b. October 8, 1763, bapt. March 18, 1764. Spon: Parents.
John Conrad, son of Peter Weckerle and Catharine Margaret, b. February 15, 1764, bapt. March 22, 1764. Spon: John Conrad Kerbach and wife Christine grandparents.
Maria Catharine, daughter of Herman Orner and Anna Margaret, b. September 20, 1763, bapt. April 8, 1764. Spon: Conrad Schutz and wife Maria Catharine.
Anna Catharine, daughter of Adam Schneider and Anna Catharine, b. December 5, 1763, bapt. April 8, 1764. Spon: Jacob Collman and wife, in place of her daughter.
Anna Elizabeth, daughter of Henry Weidner and Catharine Elizabeth, b. September 6, 1763, bapt. April 8, 1764. Spon: Parents.
Peter, son of Henry Strauch and Anna Maria, b. March 19, 1764, bapt. April 16, 1764. Spon: Peter Mayer and wife Anna Judith.
Susanna, daughter of William Spira and Maria, b. February 28, 1764, bapt. April 23, 1764. Spon: Jacob Gabel and Juliana Theiss.
Jane, daughter of Peter Frank and Anna Maria, b. December 24, 1763, bapt. May 6, 1764. Spon: Parents.
Anna, daughter of David Underbiler and Anna, b. May 1, 1764, bapt. May 20, 1764. Spon: Jacob Mayer and wife Anna.
Elizabeth Gertrude, daughter of John Gerlach Bornhütter and Elizabeth Catharine, b. April 16, 1764, bapt. June 3, 1764. Spon: Balthasar Christ and wife Elizabeth Gertrude.
Susanna, daughter of Philip Dotterer and Janike (Jeanette), b. October 18, 1763, bapt. June 29, 1764. Spon: Henry Dotterer and Susanna Gysbert, single.
Henry, son of Daniel Kampman and Elizabeth, b. November 24, 1763, bapt. July 1, 1764. Spon: Henry Baehr and wife Verena.
Maria, daughter of Melchior Meng and Maria, b. May 1, 1764, bapt. July 1, 1764. Spon: Parents.
Maria, daughter of John Miller and Margaret, b. June 17, 1764, bapt. July 8, 1764. Spon: Parents.
Anna Susanna, daughter of John Groff and Elizabeth, b. February 24, 1764, bapt. July 23, 1764. Spon: Parents.
Maria Barbara, daughter of Henry Frey and Christine, b. April 18, 1764, bapt. July 23, 1764. Spon: Michael Theiss and wife Anna Barbara.
Daniel, son of William Kampman and Anna Catharine, b. February 18, 1764, bapt. August 12, 1764. Spon: Daniel Kampman and wife

Elizabeth.

Bernard, son of Bernard Matthaeus and Elizabeth, b. July 23, 1764, bapt. August 12, 1764. Spon: Parents.

Elizabeth, daughter of Matthew Miller and Anna Margaret, b. August 21, 1764, bapt. September 2, 1764. Spon: John Peter Bannet and wife Elizabeth.

Jacob, son of Adam Winhard and Elizabeth, b. December 20, 1763, bapt. September 2, 1764. Spon: Parents.

John, son of Peter Straub and Catharine, b. June 28, 1764, bapt. September 9, 1764. Spon: John Straub, single.

Elizabeth, daughter of John Jacob Stoth and Hannah, b. July 22, 1764, bapt. October 11, 1764. Spon: Parents.

Joseph and Benjamin, twins, sons of Jacob Hegy and Maria, b. September 19, 1764, bapt. October 12, 1764. Spon: John Rex and Sybil, and Abraham Rex and Anna.

Ludwig (Lewis), son of Conrad Roesch and Catharine, b. January 16, 1764, bapt. August 26, 1764. Spon: Ludwig Treichel and wife Elizabeth.

Jacob Daniel, son of Jacob Kuebeler and Magdalene, b. September 26, 1764, bapt. December 2, 1764. Spon: grandparents and parents.

Catharine Elizabeth, daughter of Peter Dischong and Maria, b. September 13, 1764, bapt. November 25, 1764. Spon: Godfried Lehr and wife Cath. Elizabeth, and Elizabeth Dischong, grandmother.

1765

Daniel, son of John Bockius and Elizabeth, b. October 26, 1764, bapt. January 13, 1765. Spon: Parents.

John Casper, son of Casper Hencky and Catharine, b. October 15, 1764, bapt. January 27, 1765. Spon: Casper Kies and wife Catharine.

Daniel, son of John Roboleucht and Anna Catharine, b. January 21, 1765, bapt. January 27, 1765. Spon: Daniel Hess and wife.

William, son of Christian Edel and Catharine, b. October 15, 1764, bapt. February 24, 1765. Spon: Parents.

Gerard Henry, son of Henry Schuetz and Catharine, b. December 9, 1764, bapt. March 2, 1765. Spon: Gerard Henry Schuetz and wife Elizabeth, grandparents.

Christine Barbara, daughter of Jacob Ries and Christine Dorothy, b. February 15, 1765, bapt. March 17, 1765. Spon: Anna Barbara Junk.

Christopher, son of John Weidman and Margaret, b. February 18, 1765, bapt. April 21, 1765. Spon: Christopher Weydman and wife Elizabeth.

Hester, son of Jacob Zubly and Hester, b. February 27, 1765, bapt. May 5, 1765. Spon: Jacob Madery and wife Hester, grandparents.

Margaret, daughter of Ulrich Meng and Sarah, b. ----, bapt. May 12, 1765. Spon: Parents.

John Daniel, son of Daniel Huhn and Christine, b. April 7, 1765, bapt. May 30, 1765. Spon: Parents.

Jacob, son of Jacob Braun and Magdalene, b. February 8, 1765, bapt. June 2, 1765. Spon: Jacob Mayer and wife Barbara.

John, son of John Walther and Sarah, b. May 12, 1765, bapt. June 2, 1765. Spon: John Gross and wife Elizabeth.

Henry, son of Henry Mayer and Margaret, b. August 27, 1764, bapt.

May 26, 1765. Spon: Henry Oberlaender and wife Verena.

Anthony, son of Christopher Hargischeimer and Sarah, b. May 16, 1765, bapt. June 16, 1765. Spon: Anthony Gilbert and wife Sophia.

Anna Barbara, daughter of Henry Baehr and Verena, b. March 17, 1765, bapt. June 30, 1765. Spon: Henry Kalbfleisch and wife Anna Barbara.

John George, son of Bernard Kuter and Anna Maria, b. June 24, 1765, bapt. August 9, 1765. Spon: John George Sing and wife Catharine.

Maria, daughter of Rudolph Ebrecht and Apollonia, b. May 7, 1765, bapt. August 25, 1765. Spon: Maria Petri.

Jacob, son of Jacob Schmid and Maria Eva, b. September 24, 1764, bapt. August 25, 1765. Spon: Valentine Petri and wife Sarah.

John Jacob, son of Frederick Altimus and Susanna, b. May 22, 1765, bapt. Septmeber 1, 1765. Spon: Parents.

A son of William Tustin and Elizabeth, b. August 13, 1765, bapt. October 5, 1765. Spon: Joseph Funck and ----.

Maria Magdalena, daughter of Rudolph Weiss and Anna, b. September 13, 1765, bapt. October 13, 1765. Spon: Isaac Budeman and wife Maria Magdalena.

John, son of George Sebastian Unruh and Catharine, b. October 11, 1765, bapt. October 20, 1765. Spon: John Unruh and wife Apollonia.

John George, son of George Schade and Anna Maria, b. September 12, 1765, bapt. October 20, 1765. Spon: Theobald Thiel and wife Magdalena.

Elizabeth, daughter of Rudolph Laedsch and wife, b. ----, bapt. November 7, 1765. Spon: Matthew Kern and wife.

John Matthew, son of Rudolph Zubly and Elizabeth, b. September --, 1765, bapt. November 7, 1765. Spon: Matthew Kern and wife.

John Christian, son of John Kerbach and Sybilla, b. October 6, 1765, bapt. December 27, 1765. Spon: John Christian Kerbach and wife Maria Christine.

Daniel, son of John Jacob Kerbach and Christine, b. December 9, 1765, bapt. December 27, 1765. Spon: John Daniel Huhn and wife Christine Marg.

John, son of Jacob Noll and Maria Catharine, b. December 11, 1765, bapt. December 29, 1765. Spon: John Jacob Jud and Anna Catharine Jung, single.

1766

John, son of Peter Ozias and Magdalene, b. September 6, 1765, bapt. January 1, 1766. Spon: Parents.

Anna, daughter of Peter Weckerle and Catharine Margaret, b. December 17, 1765, bapt. January 19, 1766. Spon: Rudolph Grauer and Anna Weckerle, single.

John Rudolph, son of John Sorber and Magdalene, b. January 17, 1766, bapt. January 26, 1766. Spon: Parents.

Valentine, son of Jacob Gardner and Rachel, b. ----, bapt. January 26, 1766. Spon: Valentine Klages and wife.

Jacob, son of Godfried Bockius and Philippina Cath., b. December -, 1765, bapt. February 24, 1766. Spon: Jacob Daubedistel and wife.

Maria, daughter of George Adam Karnagel and Catharine, b. June 26,

1765, bapt. March 2, 1766. Spon: Peter Dischong and wife Anna Maria Judith.

John Adam, son of Nicholas Huettel and Anna Eva Catharine, b. January 17, 1766, bapt. March 30, 1766. Spon: John Henrich and wife Maria Catharine.

Peter, son of Daniel Joost and Elizabeth of Whitpain, b. January 28, 1765, bapt. February 11, 1766. Spon: Jacob Joost and wife Sarah, grandparents.

Jacob, son of Peter Joost and Sarah, b. October 22, 1765, bapt. February 11, 1766. Spon: Jacob Joost and wife Sarah, grandparents.

Henry, son of Nicholas Kunrath and Elizabeth, b. October 14, 1765, bapt. February 11, 1766. Spon: George Kunrath and wife.

Elias, son of Jacob Surber and Anna, b. March 6, 1766, bapt. April 6, 1766. Spon: Joseph Funk and wife Magdalene.

John George, son of William Till and Anna, b. ----, bapt. April 6, 1766. Spon: Casper Sorber and wife.

A daughter of Herman Orner and Anna Margaret, b. ----, bapt. May -, 1766. Spon: Jacob Coleman and wife Eva Maria.

Margaret, daughter of Christopher Grosskopp and wife, b. January 24, 1766, bapt. May 2, 1766. Spon: George Walther and wife Margaret.

John, son of John George Alsentz, pastor loci, and Barbara, b. April 9, 1766, bapt. April 22, by Rev. Weyberg. Spon: Parents.

Maria Catharine, daughter of Jost Finke and Maria Elizabeth, b. June 5, 1766, bapt. June 28, 1766. Spon: Maria Catharine Noll.

John Peter, son of Daniel Kampman and Elizabeth, b. October 26, 1765, bapt. June 29, 1766. Spon: Henry Baehr and wife Verena.

Theobald, son of Daniel Endt and Rachel, b. January 25, 1754, bapt. April 10, 1766. Spon: ----.

Elizabeth, daughter of Nicholas Billman, dec. and Elizabeth, b. May 6, 1766, bapt. August 17, 1766. Spon: John Widmer and wife Elizabeth, grandparents.

William, son of Matthew Richard and wife, b. July 27, 1766, bapt. August 15, 1766. Spon: Parents.

A son of Frederick Meyly and Barbara, b. ----, bapt. August 7, 1766. Spon: Parents.

Elizabeth, daughter of Peter Bockius and Maria, b. March 7, 1764, bapt. August 29, 1766. Spon: Parents.

Peter, son of Peter Bockius and Maria, b. May 26, 1766, bapt. August 29, 1766. Spon: Parents.

Christine, daughter of William Kampman and Anna Catharine, b. November 30, 1765, bapt. October 12, 1766. Spon: Jacob Maurer and wife Christine.

John Jacob, son of John Weidman and Eva Margaret, b. October 4, 1766, bapt. November 23, 1766. Spon: Parents.

Peter, son of Peter Ott and Anna, b. Juy 27, 1766, bapt. November 23, 1766. Spon: Rudolph Latsch and wife.

Catharine, daughter of Daniel Haubensack and Juliana, b. September 25, 1766, bapt. December 7, 1766. Spon: John George Mayer and wife Catharine.

Matthew, son of William Tustin and Elizabeth, b. October 17, 1766, bapt. December 7, 1766. Spon: Joseph Funck and wife.

Matthew son of George Gerster and Margaret, b. October 14, 1766, bapt. December 14, 1766. Spon: Matthew Heiss and wife

Margaret, grandparents.
Susanna, daughter of Charles Wiederhold, dec. and Susanna, b. September 7, 1766, bapt. October 12, 1766 by Rev. Bucher, at Fredrickstown, on the Swatara. Spon: Mother.
Christopher, son of Joseph Bender and Catharine, b. Septemer 24, 1766, b. October --, 1766. Spon: Christopher Meng and wife Catharine.
George, son of George Armengast and Catharine, b. October 17, 1766, bapt. December 21, 1766. Spon: George Geiler and wife Barbara.
Jacob, son of Sebastian Madery and Catharine, b. July 14, 1766, bapt. December 25, 1766. Spon: Jacob Madery and wife Hester, grandparents.
John William, son of John Jacob Stoth and Anna [Hanna?] Elizabeth, b. October 31, 1766, bapt. December 25, 1766. Spon: Parents.
George, son of Christopher Hargischeimer and Sarah, b. September 16, 1766, bapt. November --, 1766. Spon: George Alsentz, p.l. and wife Barbara.
John Christopher, son of Matthew Miller and Margaret, b. November 30, 1766, bapt. December 26, 1766. Spon: Parents.
Margaret, daughter of John Miller and Margaret, b. August 24, 1766, bapt. December 26, 1766. Spon: Parents.

1767
David, son of David Ungerbiel and Anna, b. January 1, 1767, bapt. January 11, 1767. Spon: Jacob Mayer and wife Anna, grandparents.
Catharine, daughter of Henry Baehr and Margaret, b. October 12, 1766, bapt. February 19, 1767. Spon: Maria Voltz.
Anna, daughter of Henry Baehr* and Verena, b. January 7, 1767, bapt. February 19, 1767. Spon: Jacob Maurer and wife Anna.
* These two Henry Baehr are not related.
John Henry, son of Michael Klein and Elizabeth, b. November 2, 1766, bapt. February 19, 1767. Spon: Parents.
Maria Magdalena, daughter of Jacob Horder and Magdalene, b. January 30, 1767, bapt. March 1, 1767. Spon: Valentine Horder and Maria Magd. Reiss, single.
Daniel, son of John Grider and Elizabeth, b. December 22, 1766, bapt. April 19, 1767. Spon: Jacob Mayer and wife Barbara.
Elizabeth, daughter of Henry Mayer and Margaret, b. June 22, 1766, bapt. ----. Spon: Henry Oberlaender and wife Verena.
Anna Elizabeth, daughter of Adam Schneider and Anna Catharine, b. March 11, 1767, bapt. June 21, 1767. Spon: Parents.
Anna Magdalene, b. Jacob Surber, dec. Anna Surber, widow, b. June 23, 1767, bapt. July 12, 1767. Spon: Joseph Funck and wife Magdalene.
John Peter, son of Jacob Edeborn and Elizabeth, b. December 28, 1766, bapt. July 12, 1767. Spon: Jacob Enck and wife Catharine.
Magdalene, daughter of Jacob Edeborn and Elizabeth, b. June 13, 1767, bapt. July 12, 1767. Spon: ----.
Jacob, son of George Walther and Margaret, b. May 26, 1767, bapt. August 9, 1767. Spon: Parents.
Elizabeth, daughter of Peter Riddle and Catharine, b. August 23, 1767, bapt. September 13, 1767. Spon: Henry Beck and wife Elizabeth.

Baptisms of the Rev. John Christopher Faber
December 1767 - August 1768

John Jacob, son of John Christopher Grosskopp and Margaret, b. ---, bapt. December 13, 1767. Spon: Parents.

George Michael, son of Michael Schmid and Barbara, b. ----, bapt. December 27, 1767. Spon: Parents.

Anna Margaret, daughter of Simon Kukert and Anna Margaret, b. ----, bapt. December 27, 1767. Spon: Parents.

John Peter, son of Peter Straup and Catharine, b. ----, bapt. December 27, 1767. Spon: Parents.

1768

Peter, son of Peter Mayer and Anna Judith, b. September 26, 1767, bapt. January 3, 1768. Spon: Parents.

David, son of Henry Gutmann and Charlotte, b. ----, bapt. March 6, 1768. Spon: Parents.

Sophia and Catharine, daughters of Solomon Sell and Sophia, b. March 9, 1768, bapt. March 23, 1768. Spon: George Schmid and Sophia, Andrew Bauer and Catharine Reisinger.

Salome, son of Jacob Schuster and Anna Eva, b. ----, bapt. April 3, 1768. Spon: Salome Steffens and Andrew Dauber.

Septimus, son of William Dosten and Elizabeth, b. January 13, 1768, bapt. May 12, 1768. Spon: Joseph Funck and wife Maria.

Anna Margaret, daughter of Valentine Horter and Maria Madgalene, b. January 7, 1768, bapt. June 16, 1768. Spon: Anna Margaret Reis, widow of George Reis, of Kinsintaun (Kensington).

Magdalene, daughter of Jacob Faut and Louisa, b. May 22, 1768, bapt. June 19, 1768. Spon: Theobald Thiel and wife Magdalene.

Magdalene, daughter of Peter Osius and Magdalene, b. May 6, 1768, bapt. June 19, 1768. Spon: Parents.

Anna Maria, daughter of George Weber and Catharine, b. December 18, 1767, bapt. June 27, 1768. Spon: Andrew Fischer and wife Anna Maria.

Margaret, daughter of Frederick Gerster and Elizabeth, b. February 24, 1767, bapt. June 26, 1768. Spon: Margaret Ro(h)r.

Anna, daughter of Christopher Hargischeimer and Sarah, b. June --, 1768, bapt. July 3, 1768. Spon: Anna Schmid, wife of William Schmid.

George, son of George Bader and Elizabeth, b. ----, bapt. August 14, 1768. Spon: George Brunner and Veronica Meyer.

Henry, son of George Schad and Anna Maria, b. August 29, 1768, bapt. August 14, 1768. Spon: Henry Funck and wife Christine.

The next time three baptisms are by an unknown hand.

Joseph, son of Joseph Bender and wife, b. September 13, 1768, bapt. ----. Spon: Christopher Meng and wife.

Maria, daughter of Matthew Haas and wife, b. October 20, 1768, bapt. ----. Spon: Matthew Degler and Susanna Degler.

Margaret, daughter of Christian Minnich and wife, b. November 10, 1768, bapt. ----. Spon: Christian Minnich and wife.

Baptisms of the Rev. Frederick Foehring

Christine, daughter of Jacob Wunner and Maria, b. ----, bapt. April 9, 1769, 11 mos. old. Spon: ----.

Jacob, son of Jacob Nuss and Maria, b. December 2, 1768, bapt.

April 9, 1769. Spon: ----.
Elizabeth, daughter of George Unruh and Catharine, b. October 7, 1768, bapt. April 24, 1769. Spon: ----.
Maria, daughter of John Menchen and Anna, b. March 12, 1769, bapt. May 9, 1769. Spon: ----.
Elizabeth, daughter of Thomas Nunweiler and Maria Dorothea, b. February 28, 1769, bapt. May 25, 1769. Spon: ----.
Joseph, son of Henry Behr and Verena, b. April 20, 1769, bapt. June 2, 1769. Spon: ----.
Anna Maria, daughter of Andrew Summer and Eva, b. May 22, 1769, bapt. June 2, 1769. Spon: ----.
Elizabeth, daughter of William Lescher and Rachel, b. ----, bapt. June 2, 1769. Spon: ----.
Susanna, daughter of Christopher Grosskop and Margaret, b. March 12, 1769, bapt. June 18, 1769. Spon: ----.
Elizabeth, daughter of Rudolph Kroman and Catharine Eva, b. March 17, 1769, bapt. June 18, 1769. Spon: ----.
Maria Margaret, daughter of Jacob Brown and Magdalene, b. February 21, 1769, bapt. June 18, 1769. Spon: ----.
Abraham, son of Abraham Belition and Margaret, b. December 6, 1768, bapt. June 18, 1769. Spon: ----.
Elizabeth, daughter of Frederick Gerster and Elizabeth, b. February 28, 1769, bapt. June 30, 1769. Spon: ----.
Margaret, daughter of Ludwig Schneider and Catharine, b. September 7, 1767, bapt. July 2, 1769. Spon: ----.
Margaret Canada, daughter of ----, b. February 9, 1757, bapt. July 2, 1769. Spon: ----.
John Hugh, son of ----, b. May 8, 1768, bapt. July 2, 1769. Spon: ----.
David, son of Abraham Henrich and Elizabeth, b. December 25, 1768, bapt. July 15, 1769. Spon: ----.
Anthony, son of Gerhard Bornhueter and Catharine, b. December 16, 1768, bapt. July 15, 1769. Spon: ----.
Elizabeth, daughter of Jacob Kibler and Maria Magdalena, b. May 11, 1769, bapt. July 23, 1769. Spon: ----.
Maria Catharine, daughter of Michael Schneider and Sophia, b. April 10, 1769, bapt. August 13, 1769. Spon: ----.
Anna Barbara, daughter of James Kruder and Elizabeth, b. June 8, 1769, bapt. August 13, 1769. Spon: ----.
Jacob, son of Conrad Lieser and Christine, b. June 12, 1769, bapt. August 14, 1769. Spon: ----.
John, son of David Juvenal and Dorothea, b. July 14, 1769, bapt. August 16, 1769. Spon: ----.
Maria Magdalena, daughter of Valentine Horter and Maria Magdalena, b. July 14, 1769, bapt. August 27, 1769. Spon: ----.
Maria Magdalene, daughter of John Sorber and Maria Magdalene, b. August 17, 1769, bapt. August 30, 1769. Spon: ----.
Anna Margaret, daughter of Henry Baehr and Anna Margaret, b. July 12, 1769, bapt. September 17, 1769. Spon: ----.
Henry, son of Rudolph Maurer and Anna, b. September 23, 1768, bapt. September 25, 1769. Spon: ----.
Anna, daughter of Jacob Neff and Anna, b. August 10, 1769, bapt. August 25, 1769. Spon: ----.
Catharine, daughter of George Nunmacher and Catharine, b. August 17, 1769, bapt. September 27, 1769. Spon: ----.

Catharine, daughter of Balser Ruple (Rubel) and Rebecca, b. July 9, 1769, bapt. October 8, 1769. Spon: ----.
Elizabeth, daughter of John Hesler and Maria, b. September 3, 1769, bapt. October 8, 1769. Spon: ----.
Maria, daughter of Peter Bockius and Maria, b. November 28, 1768, bapt. October 11, 1769. Spon: ----.
Catharine, daughter of Jacob Karg and Anna, b. August 31, 1769, bapt. October 19, 1769. Spon: ----.
Frederick, son of Jacob Schmidt and Maria, b. February 18, 1767, bapt. November 5, 1769. Spon: ----.
John Christopher, son of Christian Gutknecht and Maria Magdalena, b. October 2, 1769, bapt. November 16, 1769. Spon: ----.
Anna Maria, daughter of Conrad Marky and Verena, b. November 10, 1769, bapt. November 19, 1769. Spon: ----.
Anna Catharine, daughter of Peter Schmidt and Maria Elizabeth, b. October 4, 1769, bapt. November 19, 1769. Spon: ----.
John Peter, son of John Jacob Stout and Anna Elizabeth, b. September 24, 1769, bapt. November 19, 1769. Spon: ----.
George, son of Jacob Horter and Magdalene, b. September 14, 1769, bapt. December 5, 1769. Spon: ----.
John, son of Conrad Bear and Catharine, b. October 20, 1769, bapt. December 10, 1769. Spon: ----.
Margaret, daughter of George Hester [Gester?] and Margaret, b. April 15, 1769, bapt. December 10, 1769. Spon: ----.
Maria, daughter of John Albert and Maria, b. November 25, 1769, bapt. December 17, 1769. Spon: ----.
Maria Barbara, daughter of Frederick Swarts and Rebecca, b. June 31, 1769, bapt. December 18, 1769. Spon: ----.
Peter, son of Peter Cocker and Margaret, b. May 4, 1769, bapt. Deember 26, 1769. Spon: ----.
George, son of Peter Straub and Catharine, b. November 2, 1769, bapt. December 26, 1769. Spon: ----.
Maria, daughter of William Spenster and Maria, b. November --, 1768, bapt. December 31, 1769. Spon: ----.

1770
John George and Bernard, sons of John Bockius and wife, b. March 13, 1769, bapt. January 1, 1770. Spon: ----.
Isaac Timber, son of --- Timber and wife, b. December 20, 1769, bapt. January 1, 1770. Spon: ----.
Susanna Magdalene, daughter of Jacob Ries and Christine Dorothy, b. January 6, 1770, bapt. January 22, 1770. Spon: ----.
William, son of Christopher Hargischeimer and Sarah, b. December 5, 1769, bapt. January 28, 1770. Spon: ----.
Barbara, daughter of Jacob Meyer and Barbara, b. January 11, 1770, bapt. January 28, 1770. Spon: ----.
Solomon, son of Solomon Sels and Sophia, b. January 24, 1770, bapt. February 4, 1770. Spon: ----.
William, son of Jacob Hoffman and Sophia, b. March 17, 1768, bapt. February 11, 1770. Spon: ----.
Charles, son of William Dasten and Elizabeth, b. September 28, 1769, bapt. February 19, 1770. Spon: ----.
John Jacob, son of John [*Jacob added by hand*] Gardiner and Regina, b. January 14, 1770, bapt. February 19, 1770. Spon: ----.

John, son of John Curwell and Anna Maria, b. September 13, 1769, bapt. February 23, 1770. Spon: Bernard Matthias and Anna Elizabeth.
Cornelius, son of Abraham Van Devender and Ariangy, b. January 12, 1770, bapt. March 5, 1770. Spon: ----.
Jacob and Paul, sons of William Townzoecht and Mary Magdalene, b. March 7, 1770, bapt. March 16, 1770. Spon: ----.
Eva, daughter of John Peter Riddle and Catharine, b. November 11, 1769, bapt. March 20, 1770. Spon: John Fry and wife Eva.
Elizabeth, daughter of Leonard Notz and Margaret, b. December 9, 1769, bapt. April 15, 1770. Spon: ----.
John, son of Henry Freily and Susanna, b. February 6, 1770, bapt. April 15, 1770. Spon: ----.
Christopher, son of Christopher Maurer and Anna, b. January --, 1770, bapt. April 16, 1770. Spon: ----.
Anna Maria, daughter of Jacob Vaut and Louisa, b. ----, 1770, bapt. April 17, 1770. Spon: ----.
Elizabeth, daughter of John Lamb and Maria, b. January 28, 1770, bapt. April 17, 1770. Spon: ----.
Philip, son of G. Sebastian Unruh, b. October 18, 1769, bapt. April 22, 1770. Spon: ----.
Phoebe, daughter of Henry Meyer and Margaret, b. August 16, 1768, bapt. May 16, 1770. Spon: ----.
John, son of Peter Degen and Catharine, b. March 16, 1770, bapt. May 21, 1770. Spon: John F. Heischler.
John, son of Jacob Kerbauch and Catharine, b. ----, bapt. May 21, 1770. Spon: ----.
Christine, daughter of Peter Weissman and Elizabeth Margaret, b. March 25, 1770, bapt. May 22, 1770. Spon: Christine Blecher.
Daniel, son of Daniel Suter and Anna Catharine, b. April 28, 1770, bapt. May 24, 1770. Spon: ----.
John Gerhard, son of Michael Alt and Maria Elizabeth, b. May 25, 1770, bapt. June 2, 1770. Spon: ----.
Anna Catharine, daughter of William Reider and Catharine, b. May 31, 1770, bapt. July 1, 1770. Spon: ----.
Adam, son of Daniel Keyser and Regina, b. December 17, 1768, bapt. July 15, 1770. Spon: Michael Alt and Maria Elizabeth.
Jacob, son of Isaac Butemong and Maria Magdalena, b. May 1, 1770, bapt. July 22, 1770. Spon: ----.
Anna Elizabeth, daughter of Henry Simons and Anna Elizabeth, b. June 17, 1770, bapt. July 29, 1770. Spon: ----.
Lovina Catharine, daughter of George Weber and Catharine, b. April 25, 1770, bapt. August 19, 1770. Spon: ----.
Anna, daughter of Henry Meier and Catharine, b. April 26, 1770, bapt. September 9, 1770. Spon: ----.
John Peter, son of John Bast and Elizabeth, b. January or February, 1770, bapt. September 14, 1770. Spon: Peter Bannot, of Phila.
Henry, son of Philip Kruetzweis and Catharine, b. September 26, 1770, bapt. October 7, 1770. Spon: ----.
Anna Maria, daughter of Casper Hinkel and Catharine, b. September 21, 1770, bapt. October 7, 1770. Spon: Godfried Hob and Anna Maria.
George Adam, son of Jacob Nuss and Anna, b. October 8, 1770, bapt. November 27, 1770. Spon: ----.
Anna Christine, daughter of Daniel Campman and Elizabeth, b. August

18, 1770, bapt. December 2, 1770. Spon: ----.
Susanna Elizabeth, daughter of Daniel Funs and Christine, b. December 1, 1770, bapt. December 25, 1770. Spon: ----.
Nicholas, son of George Nicholas Unruh and Catharine, b. June 29, 1770, bapt. December 25, 1770. Spon: ----.
David, son of Jacob Kuebler and Magdalene, b. September 20, 1770, bapt. December 26, 1770. Spon: ----.

1771
Jacob, son of Jacob Ritter and Catharine, b. November 9, 1770, bapt. January 6, 1771. Spon: ----.
Adam, son of Valentine Hang and wife, b. January 5, 1771, bapt. January 24, 1771. Spon: ----.
Jesse, son of ---- Levering and wife, b. August 14, 1767, bapt. ----. Spon: The mother, John Hinkel.
Enoch, son of ---- Levering and wife, b. July 4, 1769, bapt. ----. Spon: The mother John Hinkel.
Joseph, son of Joseph Painter and Catharine, b. November 9, 1770, bapt. January 27, 1771. Spon: ----.
Jacob, son of Matthias Hass and Susanna, b. December 17, 1770, bapt. January 27, 1771. Spon: ----.
Joseph, son of Christian Minnig and Anna, b. December 11, 1770, bapt. February 23, 1771. Spon: ----.
John, son of John Eberhard and Elizabeth, b. February 7, 1771, bapt. March 16, 1771. Spon: ----.
Elizbeth, daughter of Conrad Henrich and Maria Agnes, b. January 1, 1771, bapt. March 16, 1771. Spon: ----.
Catharine, daughter of Henry Schuetz and Catharine, b. December 18, 1770, bapt. March 17, 1771. Spon: ----.
Joanna Catharine, daughter of Michael Groff and Anna Margaret, b. October 28, 1770, bapt. April 7, 1771. Spon: ----.
Peter, son of Peter Weiss and Catharine, b. August 13, 1770, bapt. April 7, 1771. Spon: ----.
John, son of John Fries and Margaret, b. February 14, 1771, bapt. April 7, 1771. Spon: ----.
Charlotte, daughter of John George Fries and Elizabeth, b. June 23, 1770, bapt. April 9, 1771. Spon: ----.
Hannah, daughter of John Kneip and Barbara, b. March 12, 1770, bapt. April 9, 1771. Spon: ----.
Jacob, son of Felix Dutweil and Elizabeth, b. April 8, 1771, bapt. April 15, 1771. Spon: ----.
Anna Margaret, daughter of John Sorber and Anna, b. February 19, 1771, bapt. April 15, 1771. Spon: ----.
Elizabeth, daughter of Jacob Wentz and Barbara, b. March 16, 1771, bapt. April 15, 1771. Spon: ----.
Anna Elizabeth, daughter of Rudolph Zuebly and Elizabeth, b. January 17, 1771, bapt. April 21, 1771. Spon: ----.
Jacob, son of George Sched and Anna Maria, b. February 8, 1771, bapt. April 21, 1771. Spon: ----.
Maria, daughter of Casper Spies and Magdalene, b. April 1, 1771, bapt. May 19, 1771. Spon: ----.
Catharine, daughter of John Deal and Elizabeth, b. March 7, 1771, bapt. May 19, 1771. Spon: ----.
Maria, daughter of Henry Mayer and Margaret, b. September 10, 1770, bapt. May 19, 1771. Spon: ----.

Henry, son of Conrad Bare (Bear) and Anna, b. April 13, 1771, bapt. May 26, 1771. Spon: ----.
John, son of John Froelich and Christine, b. May 28, 1771, bapt. June 1, 1771. Spon: ----.
Susanna and Anna Margaret, daughters of Peter Hinckel and Elizabeth, b. January 7, 1771, bapt. June 26, 1771. Spon: ---.
Hannah, daughter of John Staadt and Maria Catharine, b. April 9, 1771, bapt. June 30, 1771. Spon: ----.
Margaret, daughter of John Sorber and Anna, b. February 19, 1771, bapt. July 1, 1771. Spon: ----.
Anna, daughter of Jacob Maurer and Christine, b. April 25, 1771, bapt. July 11, 1771. Spon: ----.
Catharine, daughter of David Mack and Anna, b. June 20, 1771, bapt. July 16, 1771. Spon: ----.
Sarah, daughter of Jacob Gerster and Sophia, b. April 11, 1771, bapt. July 16, 1771. Spon: ----.
John, son of George Coler and Rosina, b. May 15, 1771, bapt. July 29, 1771. Spon: ----.
John Peter, son of Jacob Heisler and Margaret, b. July 7, 1771, bapt. August 4, 1771. Spon: ----.
George, son of Henry Guterman and Charlotte, b. May 11, 1771, bapt. August 5, 1771. Spon: ----.
James, son of John Haslet and Mary, b. July 15, 1771, bapt. August 11, 1771. Spon: ----.
Maria Margaret, daughter of George Walter and Margaret, b. May 31, 1771, bapt. August 11, 1771. Spon: ----.
Maria Magdalena, daughter of Christopher Henritzy and Elizabeth, b. August 8, 1771, bapt. September 3, 1771. Spon: ----.
Catharine, daughter of Gerard Bornhueter and Catharine, b. May 4, 1771, bapt. September 3, 1771. Spon: ----.
Daniel, son of Michael Alt and Maria Elizabeth, b. July 18, 1771, bapt. September 8, 1771. Spon: ----.
Catharine, daughter of Valentine Horter and Magdalene, b. September 4, 1771, bapt. September 18, 1771. Spon: ----.
Catharine, daughter of Simon Christein and Sarah, b. July 12, 1771, bapt. September 29, 1771. Spon: ----.
Elizabeth, daughter of Philip Engerd and Elizabeth, b. August 25, 1771, bapt. September 30, 1771. Spon: ----.
Margaret, daughter of Casper Fries and Anna Catharine, b. September 11, 1771, bapt. September 30, 1771. Spon: ----.
Susanna, daughter of John Baus and Margaret, b. March 17, 1766, bapt. September 30, 1771. Spon: ----.
Rachel, daughter of Balthasar Ruple (Rubel) and Rebecca, b. February 14, 1771, bapt. September 6, 1771. Spon: ----.
Charlotte, daughter of Solomon Sells and Catharine, b. August 17, 1771, bapt. October 20, 1771. Spon: ----.
Henry, son of George Benner and Magdalene, b. January 27, 1771, bapt. October 29, 1771. Spon: ----.
Anna, daughter of Jacob Karch and Anna, b. September 15, 1771, bapt. December 8, 1771. Spon: Matthias Kalbfleisch and Anna Conrad.
Henry, son of John Stodt and Hannah, b. November 26, 1771, bapt. December 10, 1771. Spon: ----.
Maria, daughter of Henry Sorber and Susanna, b. October 13, 1771, bapt. December 15, 1771. Spon: ----.

Eva Catharine, daughter of Daniel Suter and Anna Catharine, b. December 14, 1771, bapt. December 20, 1771. Spon: ----.
Catharine Elizabeth, daughter of Jacob Wonner and Anna Maria, b. October 12, 1771, bapt. December 26, 1771. Spon: Peter Schaurer and Elizabeth.
Catharine, daughter of Peter Straup and Catharine, b. September 12, 1771, bapt. December 29, 1771. Spon: ----.
David, son of David Ungerbulder and Anna, b. December 13, 1771, bapt. December 29, 1771. Spon: ----.

1772
Joseph, son of Henry Froelich and Susanna, b. August 17, 1771, bapt. January 1, 1772. Spon: ----.
Samuel, son of Christian Frederick Foering, V.D.M. and Margaret, b. December 20, 1771, bapt. January 5, 1772. Spon: Parents.
Jacob, son of Jacob Hehn and Magdalene, b. December 19, 1771, bapt. January 5, 1772. Spon: Jacob Engelhart and Elizabeth.
John, son of Henry Junck and Margaret, b. October 12, 1771, bapt. February 4, 1772. Spon: ----.
Anna Maria, daughter of John Henry Schuster and Sophia, b. November 20, 1771, bapt. February 13, 1772. Spon: ----.
Margaret, daughter of Martin Miller and Susanna, b. December 14, 1771, bapt. February 13, 1772. Spon: ----.
John Jacob, son of John Krauer and Maria, b. January 23, 1772, bapt. February 13, 1772. Spon: ----.
Abraham, son of Peter Paries and Maria Magdalene, b. January 24, 1772, bapt. March 14, 172. Spon: ----.
Anna Maria, daughter of John Schubert and Elizabeth, b. November 29, 1771, bapt. March 29, 1772. Spon: ----.
Anna, daughter of John Bilby and Elizabeth, b. ----, 1752, bapt. April 4, 1772. Spon: ----.

Baptisms by the Rev. J. C. Albert Helffenstein, 1772-1776

Susanna, daughter of Matthew Muller and Anna Margaret, b. March 31, 1772, bapt. April 10, 1772. Spon: Jacob Roth and wife Susanna.
Catharine, aged 3 years and Jacob, b. St. Michael's day, 1771, daughter and son of Michael Conrad and Elizabeth, bapt. April 26, 1772. Spon: Jacob Conrad and Molly Kalbfleisch, single.
John, son of John George Schubb and Christine, b. November 8, 1771, bapt. May 3, 1772. Spon: John Schubb.
William, son of William Ernst Fehlbach and Maria Elizabeth, b. March 16, 1772, bapt. April 12, 1772. Spon: Ludwig Henrich.
John Philip, son of John Albert and Maria, b. April 17, 1772, bapt. May 10, 1772. Spon: John Philip Schmidt and Magdalene.
William, son of William Tosden (Dosten) and Elizabeth, b. December 2, 1770, bapt. May 24, 1772. Spon: Joseph Funck and Magdalene, wife.
Magdalene, daughter of William Tosden (Dosten) and Elizabeth, b. February 7, 1772, bapt. May 24, 1772. Spon: Joseoph Funck and Magdalene, wife.
Jacob, son of Christopher Herrd and Susanna, b. May 1, 1768, bapt. June 7, 1772. Spon: Jacob Strauss and Maria Barbara and Father.
Christopher, son of Christopher Herrd and Susanna, b. March 4, 1772, bapt. June 7, 1772. Spon: Jacob Strauss and Maria

Barbara and Father.
Susanna, daughter of Peter Richter and Magdalene, b. June 18, 1769, bapt. June 7, 1772. Spon: Parents.
Anna, daughter of George Waschke and Margaret, b. April 21, 1770, bapt. June 7, 1772. Spon: Parents.
John Conrad, son of John Conrad Giesler and Magdalene, b. March 26, 1772, bapt. June 11, 1772. Spon: Parents.
Maria Salome, daughter of Christopher Groskopf and Maria Salome, b. September 21, 1771, bapt. June 27, 1772. Spon: Anna Maria Groskopf.
Anna Elizabeth, daughter of Jacob Groskopf and Elizabeth, b. May 26, 1772, bapt. June 27, 1772. Spon: David Daudesman and Christine, wife.
John, son of Isaac Boudemont and Maria Magdalene, b. June 2, 1772, bapt. July 26, 1772. Spon: John Habbel and Maria Catharine, his mother.
Jacob, son of John Christian Aldimus and Catharine, b. July 2, 1772, bapt. August 23, 1772. Spon: Jacob Habbel and Anna Maria Gebhard.
Christine, daughter of Casper Cremer and Sarah, b. June 22, 1772, bapt. August 27, 1772. Spon: Parents.
Daniel, son of Daniel Kayser and Regina, b. June 22, 1772, bapt. August 29, 1772. Spon: Daniel Langsdorf.
Magdalene, daughter of Henry Oberlinder and Veronica, b. July 6, 1772, bapt. September 13, 1772. Spon: Philip Werner and Margaret.
John Peter, son of Peter Laub and Margaret, b. June 20, 1772, bapt. September 18, 1772. Spon: Peter Hamm.
Jacob, son of Jacob Riess and Christine Dorothy, b. September 9, 1772, bapt. October 4, 1772. Spon: Jacob Roth and Susanna, wife.
Maria Elizabeth, daughter of Ludwig Schneider and Catharine, b. March 31, 1772, bapt. October 7, 1772. Spon: Adam Greim and Maria Elizabeth Gnes.
John Rudolph, son of Conrad Zorn and Barbara, b. October 1, 1772, bapt. November 6, 1772. Spon: John Rudolph Sorber.
Henry, son of David Mueller and Christine, b. September 20, 1772, bapt. December 14, 1772. Spon: Henry Black and Christine, wife.
Catharine, daughter of Valentine Horder and Magdalene, b. August 14, 1772, bapt. December 27, 1772. Spon: Anna Margaret Kness.

1773
John, son of Daniel Campman and Elizabeth, b. December 29, 1772, bapt. February 5, 1773. Spon: John Albert and Maria Catharine, wife.
Jacob, son of John Trubbler and Catharine, b. October 4, 1771, bapt. April 4, 1773. Spon: Jacob Sommer and Anna Maria, wife.
Anna Maria, daughter of Jacob Sommer and Anna Maria, b. December 17, 1772, bapt. April 4, 1773. Spon: Parents.
John, son of Henry Sebold and Anna, b. January 13, 1773, bapt. April 4, 1773. Spon: Parents.
Peter, son of George Heins and Catharine, b. August 31, 1772, bapt. April 12, 1773. Spon: Peter Schauer and Anna Maria Wummer.
----, ---- of Sebastian Unruh and Catharine, b. January 13, 1773,

bapt. April 12, 1773. Spon: George Kornman and Elizabeth Simon.

Maria Esther, daughter of Jacob Faud and Louise, b. February 23, 1773, bapt. April 12, 1773. Spon: Frederick Gall and Maria Esther, wife.

Anna Maria, daughter of Jacob Sommer and Anna Maria, b. December 7, 1772, bapt. April 4, 1773. Spon: Parents.

Jacob, son of John Trubbler and Catharine, b. October ----, 1771, bapt. April 4, 1773. Spon: Jacob Sommer and Anna Maria, wife.

Joseph, son of Felix Duttweiler and Elizabeth, b. October 8, 1772, bapt. April 20, 1773. Spon: Parents.

Anna Maria, daughter of Henry Mayer and Catharine, b. December 20, 1771, bapt. May 2, 1773. Spon: Parents.

Maria Eva, daughter of Andrew Scherer and Catharine, b. March 30, 1773, bapt. May 4, 1773. Spon: Philip Scherer and Maria Eva, wife.

Sarah, daughter of Henry Mayer and Margaret, b. August 22, 1772, bapt. May 30, 1773. Spon: Henry Oberlaender and Veronica, wife.

Christine Margaret, daughter of Daniel Hun and Christine Margaret, b. May 4, 1773, bapt. August 15, 1773. Spon: Parents.

Anna Barbara, daughter of John Will and Anna Maria, b. July 15, 1773, bapt. August 20, 1773. Spon: Anna Barbara Kries.

Jacob, son of Jacob Horder and Magdalene, b. February 10, 1773, bapt. June 10, 1773. Spon: Parents.

Maria, daughter of Jacob Barral and Maria, b. August 27, 1773, bapt. September 12, 1773. Spon: Parents.

Maria Eva, daughter of Peter Dedier and Maria Eva, b. June 21, 1773, bapt. July 12, 1773. Spon: Jacob Barrel and Maria, wife.

Peter, son of Daniel Reiss and Anna Catharine, b. October 13, 1773, bapt. October 12, 1773. Spon: Peter Kniess.

John George, son of Henry Simon and Anna Elizabeth, b. December 4, 1773, bapt. December 25, 1773. Spon: John George Schmidt and Elizabeth, wife.

Ludwig, son of Albertus Helffenstein (p.t. pastor) and Catharine, b. December 7, 1773, bapt. December 19, 1773. Spon: Ludwig Karcher and Marianna.

Samuel, son of Paul Groskopf and Sybilla, b. November 19, 1773, bapt. December 20, 1773. Spon: Parents.

Joseph, son of Christopher Groskopf and Margaret, b. September 11, 1773, bapt. December 20, 1773. Spon: Parents.

1774

William, son of Dewald End and Margaret, b. January 15, 1763, bapt. January 7 1774. Spon: Parents.

Bernard, son of Dewald End and Margaret, b. December 15, 1764, bapt. January 7, 1774. Spon: Parents.

Charles (Carl), son of Dewald End and Margaret, b. May 14, 1767, bapt. January 7, 1774. Spon: Charles Hau and wife.

Maria, daughter of Dewald End and Margaret, b. March 10, 1769, bapt. January 7, 1774. Spon: Parents.

Salome, son of Dewald End and Margaret, b. May 2, 1771, bapt. January 7, 1774. Spon: Parents.

Sylilla, daughter of Dewald End and Margaret, b. July 5, 1773, bapt. January 7, 1774. Spon: Parents.

"All these children belong to a man, who was a free thinker, but who begins now to adhere to our Reformed church. The two eldest sons are the children of the first wife. All the rest the children of the second wife."

Anna, daughter of Peter Huenckel and Elizabeth, b. August 29, 1773, bapt. February 7, 1774. Spon: Parents.
Anna Maria, daughter of Nicholas Schreiner and Maria, b. December 2, 1773, bapt. February 14, 1774. Spon: Christopher Meng and Catharine, wife.
Frederick, son of John Jacob Staud and Elizabeth, b. December --, 1773, bapt. March 19, 1774. Spon: Parents.
Maria, daughter of Henry Beck and Elizabeth, b. March 11, 1774, bapt. March 21, 1774. Spon: Parents.
Samuel, son of John Metzler and Louise, b. August 21, 1768, bapt. March 27, 1774. Spon: Parents.
A child of John Metzler and Louise, b. December 5, 1773, bapt. March 27, 1774. Spon: Parents.
Silas, son of John Engle and Anna, b. April 12, 1765, bapt. March 27, 1774. Spon: Parents.
Susanna daughter of John Engle and Anna, b. December 14, 1768, bapt. March 27, 1774. Spon: Parents.
John Michael, son of Matthew Zimmerle and Regina, b. March 12, 1774, bapt. April 3, 174. Spon: Michael Kuns and Anna Maria, wife.
Margaret, daughter of Peter Straub and Catharine, b. January 31, 1774, bapt. April 4, 1774. Spon: Michael Blocker and Margaret, wife.
John Conrad, son of John Zebeli and Elizabeth, b. October 1, 1773, bapt. April 4, 1774. Spon: Ulrich Mercki and Veronica, wife.
Conrad, son of Henry Baer and Catharine, b. January 22, 1774, bapt. April 17, 1774. Spon: Conrad Baer and Margaret, wife.
Elizabeth, daughter of Philip Jacob and Catharine, b. March 12, 1774, bapt. April 24, 1774. Spon: Elizabeth Schmid, single.
Sarah, daughter of Leonard Notz and Margaret, b. December 31, 1771, bapt. June 26, 1774. Spon: Parents.
Christine, daughter of Leonard Notz and Margaret, b. April 3, 1774, bapt. June 26, 1774. Spon: Parents.
Catharine, daughter of Frederick Scheibe and Barbara, b. December 10, 1773, bapt. July 10, 1774. Spon: Parents.
Elizabeth, daughter of John Stueber and Elizabeth, b. August 13, 1773, bapt. July 24, 1774. Spon: Casper Fries and Catharine, wife.
Peter, son of William Rübenkam and Anna, b. September 1, 1770, bapt. July 29, 1774. Spon: Parents.
John Michael, son of Michael Simon and Anna, b. June 28, 1774, bapt. July 29, 1774. Spon: Parents.
William, son of Jacob Sommer and Anna Maria, b. February 12, 1774, bapt. July 31, 1774. Spon: Parents.
Henry, son of Joseph Georg and Barbara, b. February 28, 1774, bapt. July 31, 1774. Spon: Parents.
Jacob, son of Jacob Ebrecht and Anna, b. January 30, 1774, bapt. August 7, 1774. Spon: Rudolph Ebrecht and Apollonia, wife.
Margaret, daughter of Henry Froelich and Susanna, b. February 9, 1773, bapt. August 10, 1774. Spon: Joseph Bender and

Catharine, wife.

Samuel, daughter of Felix Duttweiler and Elizabeth, b. August 3, 1774, bapt. August 23, 1774. Spon: Parents.

Christine, daughter of Conrad Siser and Christine, b. January 2, 1774, bapt. August 28, 1774. Spon: Jacob Maurer and Christine, wife.

Jacob, son of Henry Schlatter and Anna Maria, b. January 20, 1774, bapt. August 28, 1774. Spon: Jacob Maurer and Christine, wife.

Catharine, daughter of Michael Alt and Maria Elizabeth, b. July 4, 1773, bapt. September 7, 1774. Spon: Parents.

Charles, son of Charles Bensel and Margaret, b. May 28, 1774, bapt. September 11, 1774. Spon: Mother.

John, son of John Jacob Gardner and Rachel, b. February 12, 1772, bapt. November 13, 1774. Spon: Parents.

Henry, son of Henry Sorber and Susanna, b. October 29, 1774, bapt. November 27, 1774. Spon: Casper Sorber and Barbara, wife.

Eva, daughter of Casper Friess and Catharine, b. November 9, 1774, bapt. December 8, 1774. Spon: Frederick Muller and Eva, wife.

Susanna, daughter of George Walter and Margaret, b. October 18, 1774, bapt. December 18, 1774. Spon: Parents.

Susanna, daughter of Valentine Horder and Maria Magdalena, b. September 27, 1774, bapt. December 25, 1774. Spon: Anna Margaret Reiss.

John Frederick, son of Conrad Maurer and Philippina, b. October 8, 1774, bapt. November 6, 1774. Spon: John Frederick Dickenschied and Veronica, wife.

1775

Elizabeth, daughter of Frederick Wier and Gertrude, b. December 15, 1774, bapt. January 1, 1775. Spon: Bernard Matthias and Elizabeth, wife.

William, son of David Mack and Anna, b. October 16, 1774, bapt. January 4, 1775. Spon: Parents.

John, son of Jacob Ringer and Margaret, b. December 19, 1774, bapt. January 29, 1775. Spon: Anna Glaser.

Catharine, daughter of Joseph Bender and Catharine, b. November 16, 1774, bapt. February 27, 1775. Spon: Christopher Meng and Catharine, wife.

Margaret, daughter of Gerard Bornhüter and Catharine, b. February 1, 1775, bapt. March 4, 1775. Spon: Parents.

John, son of Peter Dedier and Margaret, b. January 30, 1775, bapt. March 15, 1775. Spon: Parents.

Daniel, son of Daniel Campman and Elizabeth, b. February 25, 1775, bapt. March 12, 1775. Spon: Casper Gunkel and Catharine.

Elizabeth, daughter of George Schaed and Anna Maria, b. July 15, 1775[1774?], bapt. April 17, 1775. Spon: Barbara Bender.

Samuel, son of Albert Helffenstein and Catharine, b. April 17, 1775, bapt. April 23, 1775. Spon: Ludwig Karcher and Mariana, wife.

John, son of Michael Forner and Maria, b. March 4, 1775, bapt. April 20, 1775. Spon: Christopher Benner and Dorothea, wife.

Magdalene, daughter of George Nicholas Unruh and Catharine, b. August 7, 1774, bapt. April 30, 1775. Spon: Parents.

John Charles, son of George Gleim and Anna Maria, b. April 7, 1775, bapt. May 7, 1775. Spon: Parents.

Louise, daughter of George Heintzel and Catharine, b. January 7, 1775, bapt. April 5, 1775. Spon: Jacob Faud and Louise, wife.
George, son of Isaac Boudemont and Magdalene, b. May 15, 1774, bapt. April 9, 1775. Spon: Parents.
George, son of Daniel Riess and Maria, b. May 28, 1775, bapt. July 2, 1775. Spon: Parents.
Susanna, daughter of Thomas Armstrong and Ella (Aelli), b. June 2, 1775, bapt. July 3, 1775. Spon: Bernard Matthias and Elizabeth, wife.
Aelli, daughter of Thomas Armstrong and Ella (Aelli), b. June 2, 1775, bapt. July 3, 1775. Spon: Bernard Matthias and Elizabeth, wife.

The following children were omitted by the Rev. Mr. Helffenstein. Entered by the Rev. Samuel Dubendorff.
Jacob, son of John Redebach and Magdalene, b. September 1, 1775, bapt. October 29, 1775. Spon: Parents.
Jacob, son of Jacob Bossert and Maria, b. October 11, 1775, bapt. November 11, 1775. Spon: David Douvenal and Dorothea, wife.
Philip, son of John Jacob Matthaeus and Catharine, b. Augut 16, 1775, bapt. November 17, 1775. Spon: Philip Conrad and Catharine, wife.
John, son of Christopher Maurer and Anna, b. November 24, 1771, bapt. December 14, 1775. Spon: Parents.

1776
Jacob, son of Jacob Sommer and Anna Maria, b. May 9, 1771, bapt. January 21, 1776. Spon: Parents.
Susanna, daughter of Philip Bayer and Catharine, b. February 24, 1775, bapt. January 21, 1776. Spon: Parents.
Susanna, daughter of Joseph George and Barbara, b. November 19, 1775, bapt. January 21, 1776. Spon: Parents.
Elizabeth, daughter of Henry Froelich and Susanna, b. January 30, 1775, bapt. January 21, 1776. Spon: Parents.
Maria, daughter of Ulrich Freyhoffer and Margaret, b. March 9, 1775, bapt. January 21, 1776. Spon: Parents.
Adam, son of Nicholas Schreiner and wife, b. January 25, 1776, bapt. March 10, 1776. Spon: Christopher Merx and wife.
John, son of ---- Geissel and wife, b. March 11, 1776, bapt. March 24, 1776. Spon: Parents.
Elizabeth, daughter of John Schuppert and wife, b. September 18, 1773, bapt. March 24, 1776. Spon: George Schneck and wife.
John, son of Daniel Sutter and Anna Catharine, b. May 8, 1776, bapt. May 14, 1776. Spon: Parents.
John George, son of John Schuppert and wife, b. January 20, 1776, bapt. May 24, 1776. Spon: Parents.
Margaret, daughter of Jacob Faut and Louisa, b. April 12, 1776, bapt. May 26, 1776. Spon: Jacob Schwefel and Margaret, wife.
Sebastian, son of Sebastian Unruh and Catharine, b. June 9, 1775, bapt. September 8, 1776. Spon: Parents.
Sarah, daughter of Christopher Hergersheimer and Sarah, b. May 20, 1776, bapt. September 8, 1776. Spon: Parents.
John Valentine, son of Valentine Horder and Magdalene, b. September 1, 1776, bapt. September 8, 1776. Spon: Parents.
George Michael, son of Peter Straub and Catharine, b. August 17,

1776, bapt. September 8, 1776. Spon: Michael Klovert and Margaret, wife.
Joseph, son of William Dosten and Elizabeth, b. September 1, 1773, bapt. September 8, 1776. Spon: Parents.
Charles, son of William Dosten and Elizabeth, b. January 18, 1775, bapt. September 8, 1776. Spon: Parents.
Henry, son of Jacob Gaertner and Regina, b. January 24, 1776, bapt. September 8, 1776. Spon: Parents.
Margaret, daughter of John Stuber and Elizabeth, b. February 13, 1776, bapt. September 9, 1776. Spon: Margaret Koeller, single.

Rev. Mr. Wack baptized during the vacancy the following (entered by Mr. Dubendorff):
Daniel, son of Henry Sorber and Susanna, b. July 23, 1776, bapt. December 22, 1776. Spon: Casper Sorber and Barbara, grandparents.
Charles, son of Paul Schuster and Margaret, b. August 22, 1776, bapt. December 22, 1776. Spon: Parents.
Peter, son of Jacob Barral and Maria, b. November 12, 1776, bapt. December 22, 1776. Spon: Parents.
Peter, son of Peter Detier and Maria, b. September 30, 1776, bapt. December 22, 1776. Spon: Parents.
Henry, son of Henry Froelich and Susanna, b. July 4, 1776, bapt. December 22, 1776. Spon: Parents.
As it may be surmised that during the vacancy and before the next pastor began his ministry, some other children may be missing...

"The following were baptized by me, the Rev. Samuel Dubendorff."

1777
Samuel, son of Jacob Bay and Christine, nee Ferner, b. April 5, 1777, bapt. May 25, 1777. Spon: The grandmother, Mrs. Glaser.
Leonard, son of Jacob Rieger and Margaret, nee Bay, b. April 6, 1777, bapt. May 25, 1777. Spon: The grandmother, Widow Bay.
Jacob, son of Casper Meier and Anna Maria, nee Haas, b. April 5, 1777, bapt. May 25, 1777. Spon: Adam Haas and wife, grandparents.
Samuel, son of John Meier and Barbara, b. September 9, 1776, bapt. June 4, 1777. Spon: Parents.
Maria Elizabeth, daughter of Daniel Reuss and Anna Catharine, b. April 7, 1775, bapt. June 4, 1777. Spon: ----.
Jacob, son of Daniel Reuss and Anna Catharine, b. February 21, 1777, bapt. June 4, 1777. Spon: ----.
Henry, son of William Freund and Sophia, nee Ernst, b. February 1, 1775, bapt. June 22, 1777. Spon: ----.
Joseph, son of Francis William Bockius and Susanna, nee Mueller, b. October 15, 1776, bapt. June 29, 1777. Spon: The grandparents of both sides.
Elizabeth, daughter of Joseph Bender and Catharine, nee Froelich, b. February 12, 1777, bapt. July 20, 1777. Spon: Parents.
Maria Catharine, daughter of Jacob Bossert and Anna Maria, nee Frey, b. July 12, 1777, bapt. August 10, 1777. Spon: ----.
Anna Elizabeth, daughter of George Gleim and Anna Maria, nee Gebhardt, b. July 11, 1777, bapt. August 31, 1777. Spon: Elizabeth Matthaeus, grandmother.

Anna Maria, daughter of Henry Brunner and Margaret, nee Keyser, b. September 22, 1777, bapt. November 2, 1777. Spon: George Brunner, brother of father, and wife.
Henry, son of Henry Keyser and Barbara, nee Loesch, b. November 21, 1777, bapt. December 1, 1777. Spon: The grandmother.
John, son of Mr. Loesch's negro, the mother's name Johannsen, b. ----, bapt. December 1, 1777. Spon: The grandmother.
Elizabeth, daughter of Stephan Feil and Elizabeth, nee Dauterman, b. November 27, 1777, bapt. December 14, 1777. Spon: Henry Blecker and wife Barbara, nee Pfaff.
John George and Henry, sons of Stephan Feil and Elizabeth, nee Dauterman, b. November 27, 1777, bapt. December 14, 1777. Spon: ----.
Three healthy and well-formed children were born to these parents on the same day.
Anna Maria, daughter of George Wunder and Anna, b. June 21, 1777, bapt. ----. Spon: Father.

1778
Elizabeth, daughter of Peter Schaurer and Apollonia Schaurer, b. ----, bapt. January 4, 1778. Spon: The mother's parents.
Catharine, Susanna, and William, children of Casper Spiess and Magdalene, nee Leitich, b. ----, bapt. January 4, 1778. Spon: The parents.
Margaret, daughter of Henry Jung and Elizabeth, nee Roher, b. December 25, 1777, bapt. January 17, 1778. Spon: Grandparents of the mother.
John, son of John Bergenhoff and Maria Margaret, b. October 7, 1777, bapt. February 2, 1778. Spon: Parents.
Catharine, daughter of Solomon Sell and Catharine, nee Seit, b. August 29, 1777, bapt. February 22, 1778. Spon: ----.
Elizabeth, daughter of Carl Frederick Hensell and Anna Margaret, nee Seit, b. January 29, 1778, bapt. February 22, 1778. Spon: ----.
Leonard, son of Leonard Notz and Margaret, nee Keyser, Luth., b. December 23, 1775, bapt. March 1, 1778. Spon: ----.
William, son of Leonard Notz and Margaret, nee Keyser, Luth., b. November 23, 1777, bapt. March 1, 1778. Spon: ----.
Maria Eva, daughter of Matthew Diel and Catharine, nee Kraut, b. November 23, 1777, bapt. March 8, 1778. Spon: ----.
John, son of John Henry Schlotter and Anna Maria, nee Reff, b. January 8, 1778, bapt. March 11, 1778. Spon: ----.
Elizabeth Maria, daughter of John Ernst Kreiss and Anna Catharine, nee Schlotter, b. February 3, 1778, bapt. March 11, 1778. Spon: ----.
Philip, son of Philip Rierig and Elizabeth, nee Strom, Luth., b. September 7, 1777, bapt. March 30, 1778. Spon: ----.
John Henry, son of John Henry Holtz and Susanna, nee Kropp, b. January 22, 1778, bapt. April 20, 1778. Spon: ----.
Michael, son of Matthias Fering and Anna Christine, nee Kremer, b. August 25, 1775, bapt. April 26, 1778. Spon: ----.
Jacob, son of Matthias Fering and Anna Christine, nee Kremer, b. April 6, 1778, bapt. April 26, 1778. Spon: ----.
Jacob, son of Casper Hefft and Maria, nee Richter, b. February 2, 1776, bapt. April 30, 1778. Spon: ----.

Michael, son of Casper Hefft and Maria, nee Richter, b. December 4, 1777, bapt. April 30, 1778. Spon: ----.

John Philip, son of Adam Lange and Catharine, nee Bröser, b. April 19, 1778, bapt. May 10, 1778. Spon: Philip Weitzel and Catharine Wagner.

Martin, son of Francis Braunholtz and Anna Barbara, nee Waltz, b. November 26, 1777, bapt. May 31, 1778. Spon: Parents.

John, son of Henry Henrici and Catharine, nee Rister, b. March 19, 1778, bapt. June 8, 1778. Spon: Father's bro. and wife.

Anna Barbara, daughter of John Herner and Anna Rosina, nee Redebach, b. December 16, 1777, bapt. July 5, 1778. Spon: Parents.

Jacob, son of John Miller and Margaret, nee Cammel, b. February 26, 1769, bapt. July 12, 1778. Spon: ----.

John, son of John Miller and Margaret, nee Cammel, b. May 4, 1771, bapt. July 12, 1778. Spon: ----.

Peter, son of John Miller and Margaret, nee Cammel, b. December 26, 1773, bapt. July 12, 1778. Spon: ----.

Eleonora, daughter of John Miller and Margaret, nee Cammel, b. March 8, 1776, bapt. July 12, 1778. Spon: ----.

George Washington, son of Theobald End and Maria, nee Haas, b. November 29, 1777, bapt. July 12, 1778. Spon: ----.

Philippina Catharine, daughter of Francis William Bockius and Susanna, nee Mueller, b. April 3, 1778, bapt. July 26, 1778. Spon: Grandparents.

Jacob and Catharine, twins of John Jacob Staat and Hannah Elizabeth, nee Heffterich, b. May 9, 1778, bapt. July 31, 1778. Spon: Parents.

Maria, daughter of Adam Becker and Elizabeth, nee Neff, b. August 8, 1777, bapt. November 24, 1778. Spon: Widow Becker, father's mother.

Isaac, son of John Redebach and Mary Magdalene, nee Betillion, b. September 27, 1778, bapt. December 6, 1778. Spon: Parents.

1779

Anna Maria, daughter of Paul Schuster and Margaret, nee Geilinger, b. October 13, 1778, bapt. February 21, 1779. Spon: Parents of father.

Catharine, daughter of John Jacob Gaertner and Regina, nee Froelich, b. September 26, 1778, bapt. February 28, 1779. Spon: Joseph Bender and wife.

George, son of Peter Detier and Maria Eva, nee Raupp, b. November 27, 1778, bapt. March 14, 1779. Spon: Parents.

John Jacob, son of John Meier and Barbara, nee Mercki, b. September 12, 1778, bapt. May 23, 1779. Spon: Grandparents.

Joseph, son of Christopher Heigersheimer and Sarah, nee Gilbert, b. February 21, 1779, bapt. May 23, 1779. Spon: Joseph Bender and wife.

John George, son of John Schuster and Elizabeth, nee Schmidt, b. May 17, 1779, bapt. June 21, 1779. Spon: Grandparents.

A child of Henry Froelich and Susanna, nee Reiss, b. February 23, 1778, bapt. June 21, 1779. Spon: Joseph Bender and wife.

Elizabeth Gertrude, daughter of Jacob Welcker and Gertrude, nee Eichacker, b. May 3, 1779, bapt. June 22, 1779. Spon: Son and wife.

Barbara, daughter of William Rittenhausen and Susanna, nee Buchmann, b. June 15, 1761, bapt. June 23, 1779. Spon: Mother.

Baptisms by the Rev. J. C. Albert Helffenstein, 1779 - 1790

John Adam, son of Peter Froelich and Maria, bapt. June 22, 1779, bapt. July 25, 1779. Spon: Philip Conrad and Catharine, wife.

Anna Barbara, daughter of Conrad Baer and Catharine, b. May 29, 1779, bapt. August 8, 1779. Spon: Nicholas Staud and Barbara, wife.

Susanna, daughter of Casper Mayer and Anna Maria, b. July 17, 1779, bapt. August 15, 1779. Spon: Parents.

Anna Elizabeth, daughter of Henry Strauss and Barbara, b. May 29, 1779, bapt. August 21, 1779. Spon: George Dannhauer and Elizabeth, wife.

Magdalene, daughter of John Wentzel and Christine, b. October 15, 1779, bapt. October 17, 1779. Spon: Philip Wentzel and Christine, wife.

Christine, daughter of Jacob Rieger and Maria, b. October 25, 1779, bapt. October 31, 1779. Spon: Jacob Bop(?) and Christine, wife.

John, son of John Walter and Elizabeth, b. October 27, 1779, bapt. November 8, 1779. Spon: John Wickerd and Hannah, wife.

John, son of Henry Brunner and Margaret, b. September 26, 1779, bapt. November 8, 1779. Spon: Parents.

Anna Maria, daughter of Michael Hahn and Catharine, b. October 15, 1779, bapt. November 14, 1779. Spon: Balthasar Hess and Anna Maria, wife.

Fransciscus, child of Peter Thiel and Catharine, b. June 24, 1779, bapt. July 1, 1779. Spon: Parents.

Adam, son of Daniel Huhn and Christine, b. October 14, 1778, bapt. June 6, 1779. Spon: Adam Schneider and Anna Marg., wife.

These two baptisms were overlooked by Dubendorff.

Jacob, son of George Wunter and Anna, b. September 5, 1779, bapt. ----. Spon: Parents.

1780

Anna, daughter of Joseph Bender and Christine, b. December 29, 1779, bapt. January 6, 1780. Spon: Parents.

Anna Margaret, daughter of Peter Worth and Eva Maria, b. October 24, 1779, bapt. January 30, 1780. Spon: Adam Schneider and Anna Margaret, wife.

John Daniel, son of Adam Schneider and Anna Margaret, b. May 19, 1779, bapt. January 30, 1780. Spon: Daniel Huhn and Christine, wife.

Sarah, daughter of Henry Mayer and Catharine, b. February 16, 1777, bapt. March 28, 1780. Spon: Parents.

Esther, daughter of Henry Mayer and Catharine, b. December 7, 1779, bapt. March 28, 1780. Spon: Parents.

Elizabeth, daughter of Jacob Anrath and Catharine, b. May 24, 1777, bapt. March 28, 1780. Spon: Parents.

Jacob Conrad, son of Jacob Anrath and Catharine, b. August 10, 1779, bapt. March 28, 1780. Spon: Parents.

Margaret, daughter of Jacob Sommer and Maria, b. February 12, 1778, bapt. May 15, 1780. Spon: Parents.

William, son of Jacob Sommer and Maria, b. October 26, 1779, bapt. May 15, 1780. Spon: Parents.
Elias, son of Philip Bayer and Catharine, b. March 28, 1777, bapt. May 15, 1780. Spon: Mother.
Sarah, daughter of Joseph Georg and Barbara, b. July 10, 1779, bapt. May 15, 1780. Spon: Parents.
Thomas, son of Thomas Armstrong and Dorothea, b. January 4, 1780, bapt. May 15, 1780. Spon: Parents.
John, son of Jacob Welcker and Elizabeth, b. May 8, 1780, bapt. July 9, 1780. Spon: Parents.
Anna Maria, daughter of Henry Baer and Maria Margaret, b. April 19, 1780, bapt. August 3, 1780. Spon: Parents.
Daniel, son of Edward Jefferi and Barbara, b. September 2, 1780, bapt. October 8, 1780. Spon: Daniel Huhn and Christine, wife.
Jacob, son of Jacob Schneider and Mary Magdalene Haubtman, b. October 25, 1780, bapt. November 28, 1780. Spon: Mother.
Elizabeth, daughter of John Gettinger and Barbara, b. August 7, 1780, bapt. December 7, 1780. Spon: Parents.

1781
Anna Christine, daughter of Thomas Zeiner and Anna Maria, b. December 20, 1780, bapt. January 7, 1781. Spon: Philip Wentzel and Anna Christine.
Elizabeth, daughter of Christopher Bockius and Sybilla, b. April 24, 1780, bapt. January 20, 1781. Spon: Parents.
Joseph, son of Joseph Bender and Catharine, b. December 3, 1780, bapt. February 18, 1781. Spon: Parents.
Elizabeth, daughter of John Jacob Gardner and Regina, b. December 16, 1780, bapt. February 18, 1781. Spon: Parents.
Henry, son of Henry Schnabel and Veronica, b. January 30, 1781, bapt. March 11, 1781. Spon: Parents.
Catharine, daughter of Francis Piquone and Maria, b. December 1, 1780, bapt. March 11, 1781. Spon: John Piquone and Catharine, wife.
Anna Maria, daughter of George Kraemer and Anna Maria, b. December 6, 1780, bapt. March 11, 1781. Spon: Parents.
Anna Margaret, daughter of Peter Eschman and Anna Maria, b. January 26, 1781, bapt. April 8, 1781. Spon: Philip Kehr and Anna Margaret.
Samuel, son of John Wentzel and Elizabeth, b. April 11, 1781, bapt. May 13, 1781. Spon: Philip Wentzel and Maria, wife.
Jacob, son of Jacob Weidman and Sarah, b. June 28, 1780, bapt. June 3, 1781. Spon: Jacob Geissler.
Catharine, daughter of Daniel Weiss and Anna Catharine, b. March 24, 1779, bapt. June 6, 1781. Spon: Parents.
Daniel, son of Daniel Reiss and Anna Catharine, b. March 17, 1781, bapt. June 6, 1781. Spon: Bernard Matthias and Elizabeth, wife.
Elizabeth, daughter of Daniel Hahn and Christine, b. February 2, 1781, bapt. July 29, 1781. Spon: Parents.
Anna Maria, daughter of Christian Geissel and Magdalene, b. June 13, 1781, bapt. September 2, 1781. Spon: Balthasar Ernst and Anna Maria, wife.
John George, son of John George Ree and Catharine, b. August 12, 1781, bapt. October 28, 1781. Spon: John George Seiferheld and

Christine Elizabeth, wife.

1782

Margaret, daughter of Daniel Campman and Elizabeth, b. January 7, 1782, bapt. March 3, 1782. Spon: John Maurer and Margaret Diehl.

Jacob, son of Leonard Sommers and Elizabeth, b. February 15, 1782, bapt. April 7, 1782. Spon: Jacob Sommers and Maria, wife.

John Henry, son of Peter Weidner and Susanna, b. August 29, 1781, bapt. April 14, 1782. Spon: Henry Weidner.

John, son of John Schuster and Elizabeth, b. January 20, 1782, bapt. May 12, 1782. Spon: John Mast.

John Henry, son of Henry Henrici and Catharine, b. April 28, 1782, bapt. June 30, 1782. Spon: Henry Oberlaender and Veronica, wife.

Mary Magdalene, daughter of Jacob Schermer and Gertrude, b. July 21, 1782, bapt. August 13, 1782. Spon: Theobald Diehl and Magdalene, wife.

John Conrad, son of Philip Wagner and Anna Margaret Schnablin (Schnabel), b. August 9, 1782, bapt. September 30, 1782. Spon: John Conrad Schnabel.

Anna Maria, daughter of John Brucker and Barbara, b. August 27, 1782, bapt. November 4, 1782. Spon: John Christopher Senderling and Maria, wife.

John Philip, son of Philip Jacob and Catharine Margaret, b. May 8, 1780, bapt. November 17, 1782. Spon: Parents.

William, son of George Wunter and Anna, b. May 3, 1782, bapt. ----, 1782. Spon: Parents.

John, son of Ulrich Freyhofer and Margaret, b. November 17, 1781, bapt. November 17, 1782. Spon: Parents.

Eva Christine, daughter of John Jacob Dieder and Christine, b. June 15, 1782, bapt. December 25, 1782. Spon: Parents.

John, son of John Geddinger and Barbara, b. September 14, 1782, bapt. December 29, 1782. Spon: Parents.

Peter, son of Peter Diehl and Catharine, b. December 19, 1782, bapt. December 29, 1782. Spon: Catharine Diehl.

Anna Barbara, daughter of Bernard Schuggard and Anna Magdalene, b. September 29, 1782, bapt. December 27, 1782. Spon: Simon Schuggard and Anna Barbara.

1783

John, son of Adam Schneider and Anna Margaret, b. April 21, 1782, bapt. February 6, 1783. Spon: Parents.

George, son of Gerhard Schneider and Rebecca, b. April 17, 1782, bapt. February 6, 1783. Spon: Parents.

Elizabeth, daughter of Henry Braun and Catharine, b. December 23, 1782, bapt. March 3, 1783. Spon: Henry Simon and Elizabeth, wife.

Joseph, son of Christopher Osias and Elizabeth, b. November 18, 1782, bapt. March 16, 1783. Spon: Joseph Biquone and Catharine Biquone.

John, son of John Wentzel and Elizabeth, b. February 15, 1783, bapt. March 23, 1783. Spon: John Froelich and Sybilla Baselman.

Michael, son of Peter Schaarer and Catharine, b. March 9, 1783, bapt. April 2, 1783. Spon: Parents.

George, son of Jacob Schasser and Anna, b. January 23, 1783, bapt. April 6, 1783. Spon: Parents.

Leonard, son of Leonard Mertz and Anna, b. December 12, 1782, bapt. April 20, 1783. Spon: Parents.

Magdalene, daughter of Henry Baehr and Margaret, b. November 10, 1782, bapt. May 11, 1783. Spon: Magdalene Schmid.

John George, son of Peter Eschman and Anna Maria, b. October 5, 1782, bapt. November 16, 1783. Spon: John George Schiefel and Anna, wife.

Samuel, son of Edward Jafferes and Barbara, b. May 14, 1783, bapt. December 13, 1783. Spon: Daniel Huhn and Christine, wife.

1784

Catharine, daughter of Benjamin Miller and Magdalene, b. December 31, 1783, bapt. March 21, 1784. Spon: Michael Kanckel and Catharine, wife.

Christine, daughter of John Peter Fuchs and Anna Maria, b. February 20, 1784, bapt. March 25, 1784. Spon: Andrew Raader and Christine, wife.

Anna, daughter of John Sorber and Margaret, b. October 1, 1783, bapt. May 2, 1784. Spon: Parents.

Juliana, daughter of George Philippi and Elizabeth, b. November 29, 1783, bapt. May 30, 1784. Spon: Bernard Mayer and Catharine, wife.

Anna, daughter of Henry Henrici and Catharine, b. May 10, 1784, bapt. June 4, 1784. Spon: Leonard Rauch and Anna, wife.

Susanna, daughter of Nicholas Muehlhaus and Juliana, b. February 2, 1784, bapt. June 5, 1784. Spon: William Holwi and Susanna, wife.

Nancy, daughter of Bernard Ward and Sarah, b. January 7, 1784, bapt. June 8, 1784. Spon: Parents.

Sarah, daughter of Jacob Froelich and Maria, b. January 19, 1784, bapt. June 6, 1784. Spon: Parents.

Charles, son of Peter Weidman and Susanna, b. September 11, 1783, bapt. June 13, 1784. Spon: Charles Mohr.

Elizabeth, daughter of Peter Dedier and Anna Eva, b. November 11, 1783, bapt. June 13, 1784. Spon: Parents.

John, son of John Rohrer and Margaret, b. March 14, 1784, bapt. June 26, 1784. Spon: Parents.

William, son of Henry Jung and Elizabeth, b. May 23, 1784, bapt. June 26, 1784. Spon: Parents.

Maria Catharine, daughter of Daniel Kampman and Elizabeth, b. May 13, 1784, bapt. July 18, 1784. Spon: John Fuchs and N.C., wife.

Maria Salome, daughter of John Maass and Anna Eva, b. May 3, 1784, bapt. July 19, 1784. Spon: Jacob Schuster and Anna Eva, wife.

Maria, daughter of J. George Schuster and Barbara, b. March 19, 1784, bapt. July 19, 1784. Spon: Parents.

John Henry, son of Henry Weidner and Cath. Elizabeth, b. August 8, 1783, bapt. August 1, 1784. Spon: Valentine End and Catharine, wife.

Elizabeth, daughter of Joseph Georg and Barbara, b. February 27, 1784, bapt. August 1, 1784. Spon: Parents.

Anna, daughter of Henry Schnabel and Veronica, b. August 4, 1784,

bapt. September 12, 1784. Spon: Ulrich Weidman and Anna, wife.
John, son of John Redebach and Maria, b. February 15, 1784, bapt. October 10, 1784. Spon: Parents.

1785

John Adam, son of John Jacob Peiffer and Catharine, b. October 26, 1784, bapt. January 1, 1785. Spon: Adam Stoll and Christine Peiffer.
John Peter, son of John Schlatter and Ann Magdalene, b. October 14, 1784, bapt. January 9, 1785. Spon: John Peter Sauer(?) and Eva, wife.
Anna, daughter of George Hacker and Maria, b. January 1, 1782, bapt. March 27, 1785. Spon: Parents.
Charles, son of George Francis and Susanna, b. October 14, 1784, bapt. March 27, 1785. Spon: Parents.
Maria Anna, daughter of George Francis and Susanna, b. August 14, 1782, bapt. March 27, 1785. Spon: Parents.
Joseph, son of Jacob Zuber and Elizabeth, b. February 28, 1785, bapt. April 10, 1785. Spon: Jacob Barral and Catharine Hess.
Daniel, son of Peter Struber and Ernestina, b. August 29, 1784, bapt. May 1, 1785. Spon: Daniel Haegi and Catharine Rapp.
Rudolph, son of Jacob Maurer and Esther, b. March 30, 1783, bapt. May 15, 1785. Spon: Parents.
Jacob, son of John Geddinger and Barbara, b. February 10, 1785, bapt. May 16, 1785. Spon: Parents.
Maria, daughter of John George Leonhard and Christine, b. August 25, 1784, bapt. May 29, 1785. Spon: Parents.
Esther, daughter of Jacob Beck and Barbara, b. February 16, 1785, bapt. June 5, 1785. Spon: Parents.
Susanna, daughter of John Sprecher and Regina, b. May 2, 1785, bapt. June 15, 1785. Spon: Parents.
Mary Magdalene, daughter of Frederick Juncker and Anna Barbara, b. April 21, 1785, bapt. July 24, 1785. Spon: Anna Sorber.
Anna Magdalene, daughter of Leonard Sommer and Elizabeth, b. May 5, 1785, bapt. August 4, 1785. Spon: Parents.
Daniel, son of Christian Freund and Elizabeth, b. July 19, 1785, bapt. August 4, 1785. Spon: Parents.
John Henry, son of Henry Niebel and Elizabeth, b. June 19, 1785, bapt. August 6, 1785. Spon: John Niebel and Maria Agnes, wife.
Margaret, daughter of Ulrich Freyhofer and Margaret, b. December 19, 1783, bapt. August 6, 1785. Spon: Parents.
Maria Elizabeth, daughter of John Brucker and Barbara, b. April 24, 1785, bapt. August 11, 1785. Spon: Maria Elizabeth Gries.
John Jacob, son of John Dedier and Charlotte, b. May 14, 1785, bapt. August 14, 1785. Spon: Parents.
Elizabeth, daughter of John Kalbfleisch and Maria, b. February 20, 1785, bapt. August 15, 1785. Spon: John Schmid and Christine Grower.
Daniel, son of Gottfried Bockius and Eva, b. August 3, 1785, baptized August 21, 1785. Spon: Parents.
Susanna, daughter of Jacob Unrath and Catharine, b. May 15, 1781, bapt. August 26, 1785. Spon: Parents and Jacob Mayer.
Maria, daughter of Jacob Unrath and Catharine, b. December 25, 1782, bapt. August 26, 1785. Spon: Parents and Jacob Mayer.
Frederick and Sarah, children of Jacob Unrath and Catharine, b.

August 18, 1785, bapt. August 26, 1785. Spon: Parents and Jacob Mayer.
Maria, daughter of John Sorber and Margaret, b. February 22, 1785, bapt. September 18, 1785. Spon: Parents.
Anna Catharine, daughter of John Utlick and Anna Eva, b. January 18, 1784, bapt. September 20, 1785. Spon: John Schlatter and Anna Cath. Schlatter.
William, son of Sebastian Unruh and Catharine, b. April 25, 1785, bapt. September 18, 1785. Spon: Parents.
Catharine, daughter of John Biquone and Sarah, b. May 2, 1785, bapt. October 20, 1785. Spon: Parents.
Anna, daughter of John Dill and Elizabeth, b. October 4, 1776, bapt. October 4, 1785. Spon: Parents.
Elizabeth, daughter of Daniel Schneeberger and Sarah, b. September 4, 1785, bapt. October 4, 1785. Spon: Parents.
George, son of Henry Rieli and Elizabeth, b. August 10, 1785, bapt. October 9, 1785. Spon: George Reiss and Elizabeth, wife.
Barbara, daughter of Gottfried Bockius and Sarah, b. December 31, 1784, bapt. October 27, 1785. Spon: Parents.
John, son of Christopher Osias and Elizabeth, b. July 11, 1785, bapt. October 27, 1785. Spon: John Biconet.
Catharine, daughter of Peter Schaarer and Catharine, b. December 12, 1784, bapt. November 5, 1785. Spon: Parents.
Anna, daughter of John George Gloss and Anna, b. February --, 1783, bapt. November 6, 1785. Spon: Parents.
John, son of John Peter Gloss and Catharine, b. September 12, 1785 bapt. November 6, 1785. Spon: Parents.
John Jacob, son of John Schuster and Elizabeth, b. April 15, 1784, bapt. November 13, 1785. Spon: Jacob Schuster and Anna, wife.
Elizabeth, daughter of John Wentzel and Elizabeth, b. September 16, 1785, bapt. November 13, 1785. Spon: Frederick Dober and Elizabeth Edel.

1786
William, son of Jacob Rieger and Margaret, b. February 15, 1786, bapt. March 19, 1786. Spon: Parents.
Elizabeth, daughter of Valentine Schmid and Susanna, b. January 6, 1786, bapt. August 13, 1786. Spon: Parents.
Thomas, son of Casper Mayer and Anna Maria, b. January 11, 1786, bapt. April 23, 1786. Spon: Parents.
Jacob, son of Andrew Hess and Susanna, b. January 14, 1785, bapt. March 26, 1786. Spon: Parents.
Maria Margaret, daughter of Henry Baer and Maria Margaret, b. September 2, 1785, bapt. March 19, 1786. Spon: Parents.
Catharine, daughter of Joshua Metzger and Sophia, b. October 23, 1783, bapt. March 19, 1786. Spon: Parents.
Margaret, daughter of John Rohrer and Margaret, b. June 29, 1785, bapt. March 19, 1786. Spon: Parents.
Jacob, son of Theobald End and Maria, b. July 28, 1785, bapt. April 23, 1786. Spon: Parents.
George, son of Valentine Horder and Magdalene, b. May 30, 1784, bapt. April 23, 1786. Spon: Parents.
George, son of George Wunder and Anna, b. September 19, 1785, bapt. April 23, 1786. Spon: Parents.
Susanna Barbara, daughter of Leonard Nutz and Margaret, b. February

1, 1786, bapt. May 14, 1786. Spon: Parents.

Catharine, daughter of Philip Schunckel and Catharine, b. March 29, 1786, bapt. June 11, 1786. Spon: Frederick Hafner and Catharine, wife.

Joseph, son of Joseph Yorg and Barbara, b. October 24, 1785, bapt. July 2, 1786. Spon: Parents.

George, son of Jacob Lautermilch and Elizabeth, b. March 17, 1786, bapt. July 16, 1786. Spon: Parents.

Edward, son of Edward Jeffers and Barbara, b. March 25, 1786, bapt. July 30, 1786. Spon: Parents.

Maria Elizabeth, daughter of William Conrad and Maria, b. May 4, 1786, bapt. August 13, 1786. Spon: William Carle and Anna Maria, wife.

Sarah, daughter of Jacob Sommers and Anna Maria, b. May 6, 1786, bapt. September 16, 1786. Spon: Parents.

Charles, son of John Hortge and Catharine, b. August 1, 1786, bapt. September 25, 1786. Spon: Parents.

Abraham, son of Daniel Springer and Catharine, b. July(?) 15, 1786, bapt. October 1, 1786. Spon: Parents.

Anna Maria, daughter of John Schlatter and Anna Magdalene, b. August 19, 1786, bapt. October 1, 1786. Spon: Andrew Ruth and Anna Maria.

Samuel, son of Daniel Huhn and Catharine, b. July 6, 1785, bapt. October 1, 1786. Spon: Daniel Huhn and Catharine.

Maria Philippina, daughter of Jacob Stees and Maria Philippina, b. July 4, 1786, bapt. October 4, 1786. Spon: Parents.

Charles, son of Peter Simon and Elizabeth, b. September 2, 1786, bapt. October 8, 1786. Spon: Charles Renner and Catharine, wife.

Henry, son of Peter Simon and Elizabeth, b. September 5, 1781, bapt. November 8, 1786. Spon: Henry Simon and Elizabeth, wife.

Anna Regina, daughter of John Peter Fuchs and Margaret, b. November 1, 1786, bapt. December 3, 1786. Spon: Martin Strauss and Regina, wife.

John Michael, son of John Bornhueter and Margaret, b. October 19, 1786, bapt. December 17, 1786. Spon: John Michael Werner and Christine, wife.

William, son of John Schuster and Elizabeth, b. November 6, 1786, bapt. December 19, 1786. Spon: Parents.

Christine, daughter of Valentine Wunder and Magdalene, b. September 16, 1786, bapt. December 25, 1786. Spon: Anthony Hargesheimer and Christine Wunder.

1787

Anna Margaret, daughter of Henry Volck and Anna Catharine, b. December 11, 1786, bapt. January 1, 1787. Spon: Peter Schell and Eliza, wife.

Sarah, daughter of Peter Faust and Anna Maria, b. August 8, 1786, bapt. February 11, 1787. Spon: Parents.

Jacob, son of Nicholas Muehlhause and Juliana, b. November 5, 1786, bapt. March 11, 1787. Spon: Jacob Zimmerman and Anna Catharine, wife.

Rachel, daughter of George Miller and M. Marg., b. May 26, 1786, bapt. April 15, 1787. Spon: Parents.

Elizabeth, daughter of John Biquone and Sarah, b. September 24,

1786, bapt. May 20, 1787. Spon: Catharine Biquone.

Anna Elizabeth, daughter of Frederick Juncker and Barbara, b. January 18, 1787, bapt. May 27, 1787. Spon: Parents.

Anna Magdalene, b. Frederick Voelcker and Anna Elizabeth, b. January 21, 1787, bapt. May 28, 1787. Spon: John Jost Voelcker and Magdalene Anna, wife.

Catharine, daughter of Stephan Englewood and Anna, b. January 18, 1787, bapt. June 10, 1787. Spon: Parents.

Samuel, son of Henry Jung and Alice, b. May 9, 1787, bapt. June 24, 1787. Spon: Parents.

George, son of Peter Schaurer and Catharine, b. December 30, 1786, bapt. June 28, 1787. Spon: Parents.

Thomas, son of John Rohrer and Margaret, b. February 9, 1787, bapt. June 28, 1787. Spon: Thomas Schmid and Sarah Gerster.

Samuel, son of Jacob Buchi and Barbara, b. March 19, 1787, bapt. June 28, 1787. Spon: Parents.

Samuel, son of Jacob Friess and Christine, b. September 19, 1786, bapt. June 29, 1787. Spon: Parents.

Charles, son of Jacob Hofman and Sophia, b. June 15, 1780, bapt. June 28, 1787. Spon: Parents.

George, son of Jacob Hofman and Sophia, b. April 4, 1781, bapt. June 28, 1787. Spon: Parents.

Samuel, son of Jacob Hofman and Sophia, b. June 30, 1783, bapt. June 28, 1787. Spon: Parents.

John Peter, son of Peter Gloss and Catharine, b. April 13, 1787, bapt. July 8, 1787. Spon: Parents.

Jacob, son of John Sorber and Margaret, b. January 17, 1787, bapt. July 8, 1787. Spon: Parents.

George, son of Jacob Peifer and Elizabeth, b. April 28, 1787, bapt. July 15, 1787. Spon: Parents.

Magdalene, daughter of George Weil and Maria, b. May 27, 1787, bapt. August 5, 1787. Spon: Conrad Weil and Magdalene Schmid.

Jacob, son of Henry Kiehl and Elizabeth, b. February 9, 1787, bapt. August 19, 1787. Spon: Parents.

John, son of John Schmid and Elizabeth, b. January 1, 1787, bapt. August 19, 1787. Spon: Parents.

Sebastian, son of Gottfried Bockius and Salome, b. May 8, 1787, bapt. August 19, 1787. Spon: Sebastian Miller.

John, son of Joseph Biquone and Anna, b. April 11, 1787, bapt. August 19, 1787. Spon: Parents.

Bernard, son of Bernard Struber and Ernestina, b. March 14, 1787, bapt. August 20, 1787. Spon: Bernard Rapp and Catharine Rapp.

Rudolph, son of John Geddinger and Barbara, b. June 22, 1787, bapt. August 26, 1787. Spon: Parents.

Henry, son of Henry Schaefer and Elizabeth, b. August 2, 1787, bapt. September 12, 1787. Spon: John End.

Catharine, daughter of John Reed and Sybilla Catharine, b. December 24, 1784, bapt. September 12, 1787. Spon: John End.

Jacob, son of John Reed and Sybilla Catharine, b. May 13, 1787, bapt. September 12, 1787. Spon: ----.

Joseph, son of Anthony Zander and Maria, b. August 3, 1786, bapt. September 16, 1787. Spon: Joseph Fetscher and Eva, wife.

Dorothea, daughter of John Wentzel and Elizabeth, b. September 19, 1787, bapt. September 25, 1787. Spon: Parents.

Margaret, daughter of Peter Diehl and Catharine, b. March 28, 1786, bapt. December 25, 1787. Spon: Margaret Diehl and grandmother.

1788

Ludovica, daughter of Casper Mayer and Maria, b. November 11, 1787, bapt. May 12, 1788. Spon: Parents.

Christine, daughter of Henry Baer and Margaret, b. November 1, 1787, bapt. May 12, 1788. Spon: Parents.

Henry, son of George Bressler and Catharine, b. March 15, 1788, bapt. May 18, 1788. Spon: Henry Davis and Maria, wife.

Philip, son of George Miller and Magdalene, b. December 25, 1787, bapt. August 21, 1788. Spon: Parents.

Henry, son of Peter Blaecker and Hannah, b. May 22, 1787, bapt. September 5, 1788. Spon: Robert Bradly and Maria, wife.

Eva, daughter of Nicholas Schmid and Margaret, b. July 2, 1787, bapt. September 14, 1788. Spon: Parents.

Catharine Elizabeth, daughter of Christian Jung and Cath. Elizabeth, b. December 26, 1786, bapt. September 14, 1787. Spon: Parents.

Anna, daughter of Jacob Ringer and Margaret, b. June 6, 1788, bapt. October 10, 1788. Spon: Anna Jund.

John, son of Henry Davis and Maria, b. August 20, 1788, bapt. October 12, 1788. Spon: Parents.

Sarah, daughter of John Ehbrecht and Christine, b. April 18, 1788, bapt. October 12, 1788. Spon: Parents.

Catharine, daughter of John Staehr and Elizabeth, b. July 27, 1788, bapt. October 26, 1788. Spon: Mother.

Susanna, daughter of Jacob Gilbert and Maria, b. April 27, 1788, bapt. November 30, 1788. Spon: Parents.

The next two were baptisms were entered by Rev. Mr. Herman.

Sarah, daughter of Jacob Weidman and Sarah, b. February 25, 1787, bapt. ----. Spon: Parents.

Maria Sarah, daughter of Jacob Loescher and Hannah Brown, b. September 18, 1788, bapt. October 18, 1788. Spon: Lewis Brown and Sarah, wife.

1789

John, son of Christian Hess and Elizabeth, b. October 28, 1788, bapt. January 18, 1789. Spon: Michael Keyser and Catharine, wife.

Henry, son of Henry Kiehl and Elizabeth, b. September 28, 1788, bapt. January 25, 1789. Spon: Henry Hunckel and Catharine, wife.

Anna Catharine, daughter of Henry Volck and Catharine, b. January 27, 1789, bapt. February 22, 1789. Spon: Henry Kiehl and Anna Catharine, wife.

Peter, son of Peter Schaurer and Catharine, b. November 27, 1788, bapt. February 26, 1789. Spon: Parents.

John Peter, son of John Bayer and Maria, b. March 6, 1778, bapt. March 2, 1789. Spon: Parents.

John, son of John Bayer and Maria, b. October 15, 1780, bapt. March 2, 1789. Spon: Parents.

John Jacob, son of John Bayer and Maria, b. December 24, 1784, bapt. March 2, 1789. Spon: Parents.

Maria, daughter of John Bayer and Maria, b. December 29, 1787,

bapt. March 2, 1789. Spon: Parents.
Samuel, son of Christopher Bockius and Sybilla, b. August 2, 1788, bapt. March 29, 1789. Spon: Parents.
Jacob, son of Henry Duttweiler and Susanna, b. September 7, 1788, bapt. April 19, 1789. Spon: Jacob Duttweiler and Maria Schaddinger.

The following five baptisms were entered by Mr. Herman, although they occurred during the ministry of Albert Helffenstein. He died May 17, 1790 at Germantown.
John Christopher, son of Frederick Junker and Elizabeth, b. March 2[or 4?], 1789, bapt. January 2, 1790. Spon: Anna Sorber, grandmother.
Mary Magdalene, daughter of Jacob Grosskopf and Elizabeth, b. September 12, 1788, bapt. August 9, 1790. Spon: Jacob Geissel and Maria, wife.
A child of Sebastian Unruh and Catharine, b. June 19, 1788, bapt. April 29, 1789. Spon: Parents.
Sebastian, son of John Unruh and Elizabeth, b. January 4, 1789, bapt. April 29, 1789. Spon: Parents.
A child of Richard Warren and Christine, b. February 16, 1789, bapt. April 24, 1789. Spon: Philip Wentzel and Christine, wife.

Baptisms by L. Frederick Hermann, 1790-1801

1790
Aaron, son of Gottfried Bockius and Eva, b. April 30, 1790, bapt. September 19, 1790. Spon: Parents.
Deborah, daughter of Christian Gutknecht and Elizabeth, b. June 16, 1790, bapt. September 21, 1790. Spon: Parents.
Samuel, son of Jacob Staadt and Barbara, b. September 9, 1790, bapt. October 31, 1790. Spon: Parents.
Anna Maria, daughter of George Bressler and Maria Catharine, b. September 10, 1790, bapt. December 3, 1790. Spon: Parents.
Nancy, daughter of Philip Fischer and Maria, b. December 1, 1790, bapt. December 5, 1790. Spon: Catharine Cunius and Peter Lauery.
Sarah, daughter of George Leonhard and Christine, b. April 11, 1790, bapt. December 24, 1790. Spon: Father.

1791
Christine Margaret, daughter of John Gerard Huhn[Hahn?] and Maria, b. December 22, 1790, bapt. January 7, 1791. Spon: Parents.
Frederick, son of Jacob Weidman and Sarah, b. August 1, 1789, bapt. ----. Spon: Parents.
Friderica Doris, daughter of Frederick Herman, V.D.M. and Maria, b. August 26, 1788, bapt. ----, 1788. Spon: Parents.
Maria Joanna Elizabeth, daughter of Frederick Herman, V.D.M. and Maria, b. October 16, 1789, bapt. ----, 1789. Spon: Parents.
Elizabeth, daughter of Peter Thiel and Catharine, b. September 29, 1790, bapt. January 16, 1791. Spon: Parents.
Anna Cath. Henrietta, daughter of L. Frederick Herman, V.D.M. and Maria, b. January 14, 1791, bapt. March 3, 1791. Spon: Parents.
Samuel, son of John Roehrer and Margaret, b. February 18, 1790,

bapt. February 6, 1791. Spon: Parents.

Susanna, daughter of Christopher Hargerheimer and Eva, b. May 13, 1790, bapt. February 7, 1791. Spon: George Rex and Susanna.

Elias, son of Henry Sorber and wife, b. August 16, 1788, bapt. April 3, 1791. Spon: Grandparents and Joseph Bender and Catharine, wife.

Anna Elizabeth, daughter of Henry Sorber and wife, b. August 16, 1788, bapt. April 3, 1791. Spon: Grandparents and Joseph Bender and Catharine, wife.

Catharine, daughter of Henry Sorber and Eva, wife, b. August 7, 1790, bapt. April 3, 1791. Spon: Grandparents and Joseph Bender and Catharine, wife.

Catharine, daughter of Peter Blecker and Joanna, b. September 9, 1790, bapt. April 10, 1791. Spon: Catharine Altemoss and Jacob Fischer.

William, son of Edward Jefferts and Barbara, b. February 26, 1791, bapt. April 10, 1791. Spon: Parents.

Margaret, daughter of Christian Hanz and Catharine, b. November 25, 1790, bapt. April 24, 1791. Spon: Joseph Stau and Eva Rosina, wife.

Elizabeth, daughter of Valentine Wunter (Wunder) and Magdalene, b. November 4, 1790, bapt. April 24, 1791. Spon: Louis Gilliams and Elizabeth.

Susanna, daughter of Abraham Paul and Barbara, b. September 2, 1789, bapt. April 25, 1791. Spon: Parents and Susanna Paul.

Maria, daughter of Jacob Guth and Elizabeth, b. February 23, 1789, bapt. April 25, 1791. Spon: Parents.

Hannah, daughter of Henry Dottweiler and Susanna, b. November 11, 1789, bapt. May 8, 1791. Spon: Parents.

William, son of Casper Meyer and Maria, b. March 24, 1789, bapt. May 8, 1791. Spon: Parents.

Charles, son of Casper Meyer and Maria, b. April --, 1791, bapt. May 8, 1791. Spon: Parents.

Catharine, daughter of Anthony Biquone and Maria, b. April 25, 1791, bapt. May 11, 1791. Spon: John Biquone and Catharine.

Susanna, daughter of Gottfried Bockius and Sarah, b. May 1, 1791, bapt. May 11, 1791. Spon: Parents.

Charles, son of Henry Kihly and Elizabeth, b. July 13, 1790, bapt. May 12, 1791. Spon: Parents.

Margaret, daughter of John Sorber and Margaret, b. March 27, 1791, bapt. May 12, 1791. Spon: Parents.

Anna, daughter of Charles Deschler and Anna, b. March 23, 1791, bapt. May 16, 1791. Spon: Parents.

Catharine, daughter of Henry Schutz and wife, b. October 29, 1790, bapt. May 16, 1791. Spon: Parents.

Jacob, son of Philip Schinkel and Catharine, b. October 26, 1790, bapt. May 29, 1791. Spon: Parents.

John, son of John Reinerdt and Margaret, b. November 30, 1790, bapt. June 13, 1791. Spon: Abraham Kaerber and Elizabeth, wife.

Catharine, daughter of Bernard Schukel and Maria, b. February 7, 1791, bapt. June 19, 1791. Spon: Parents.

George, son of George Schoettinger and Leah, b. October 30, 1790, bapt. June 26, 1791. Spon: Parents.

Maria, daughter of John Staer and Elizabeth, b. August --, 1790,

bapt. June 26, 1791. Spon: Mother and Maria Haends(?).
Susanna, daughter of Joseph Schims and wife, b. December 10, 1789, bapt. June 26, 1791. Spon: Abraham Kerber and Elizabeth.
Anna Maria, daughter of Lawrence Trong and Catharine, b. September 28, 1790, bapt. June 26, 1790 [should read 1791]. Spon: George Braun and Anna Maria.
George, son of John Mann and Maria, b. December 29, 1790, bapt. July 10, 1791. Spon: Marg. Kettel.
Sarah, daughter of John Mann and Maria, b. August 13, 1789, bapt. July 10, 1791. Spon: Parents.
A child of Leonard Notz and wife, b. ----, bapt. July 10, 1791. Spon: Parents.
Samuel, son of George Wonter and Anna, b. March 27, 1788, bapt. July 17, 1791. Spon: Father.
Catharine, daughter of George Wonter and Anna, b. April 29, 1791, bapt. July 17, 1791. Spon: Father.
Maria, daughter of Justus Schuetz and Catharine, b. June 22, 1791, bapt. July 31, 1791. Spon: Parents.
Jacob, son of John Duttweiler and Barbara, b. November 15, 1790, bapt. July 31, 1791. Spon: Parents.
John, son of Jacob Stehs and Catharine, b. May 9, 1788, bapt. August 1, 1791. Spon: Parents.
Anna Eva, daughter of George Eschen and Salome, b. March 1, 1791, bapt. August 7, 1791. Spon: Conrad Eschen and Anna Eva Schaeffer.
Richard, son of Richard Warren and Christine, b. May 1, 1791, bapt. August 7, 1791. Spon: Parents.
Anna Barbara, daughter of George Schuster and Anna Barbara, b. December 22, 1790, bapt. August 7, 1791. Spon: Christian Hetzel and Anna Barbara.
Samuel, son of John Landenberger and Anna Maria, b. December 25, 1790, bapt. August 7, 1791. Spon: Parents.
Christian Frederick, son of Pter Umringhaus and Maria, b. July 6, 1791, bapt. August 14, 1791. Spon: Margaret Boss, grandmother of child.
Jacob, son of Peter Umringhaus and Maria, b. August 12, 1789, bapt. August 14, 1791. Spon: Parents.
Margaret, daughter of Jacob Miller and Elizabeth, b. April 2, 1789, bapt. August 15, 1791. Spon: Parents and Margaret Mueller, grandmother.
Margaret, daughter of George Miller and Mary Magdalene, b. June 29, 1790, bapt. August 15, 1791. Spon: Parents.
Daniel, son of John George Fraes and Barbara, b. January 2, 1791, bapt. August 18, 1791. Spon: Parents.
Sarah, daughter of Rudolph Froelich and Elizabeth, b. April 29, 1790, bapt. August 20, 1791. Spon: Parents.
Sarah, daughter of Anthony Hergesheimer and Christine, b. September 6, 1788, bapt. August 20, 1791. Spon: Parents.
Jacob, son of Anthony Hergesheimer and Christine, b. October 3, 1790, bapt. August 20, 1791. Spon: Parents.
Anna, daughter of Joseph Sorber and Elizabeth, b. September 17, 1786, bapt. August 20, 1791. Spon: Parents.
Henry, son of Joseph Sorber and Elizabeth, b. October 3, 1788, bapt. August 20, 1791. Spon: Parents.
Elizabeth, daughter of Joseph Sorber and Elizabeth, b. November 3,

1790, bapt. August 20, 1791. Spon: Parents.

Daniel, son of Jacob Windolph and Elizabeth, b. October 17, 1788, bapt. August 24, 1791. Spon: Parents.

Maria Margaret, daughter of Jacob Windolph and Elizabeth, b. September 5, 1790, bapt. August 24, 1791. Spon: Maria Margaret Steiner.

Jacob, son of Elizabeth Grosskopf and Jacob Geissler, b. January 5, 1791, bapt. August 28, 1791. Spon: Jacob Grosskopf and Elizabeth.

Christian, son of Jacob Geissler and Hannah, b. June 5, 1791, bapt. September 21, 1791. Spon: Christian Geissler.

John Adam, son of Adam Schlatter and Anna Magdalene, b. July 2, 1791, bapt. September 25, 1791. Spon: Elizabeth Maria Schlatter and John Adam Schlatter.

Regina, daughter of Jacob Kemmel and Anna Barbara, b. September 7, 1787, bapt. September 25, 1791. Spon: Parents.

Andrew, son of Jacob Kemmel and Anna Barbara, b. November 30, 1790, 1787, bapt. September 25, 1791. Spon: Parents.

Samuel, son of Joseph Kemmel and Elizabeth, b. November 7, 1784, bapt. September 25, 1791. Spon: Parents.

Jacob, son of Joseph Kemmel and Elizabeth, b. March 18, 1787, bapt. September 25, 1791. Spon: Parents.

Sarah, daughter of Joseph Kemmel and Elizabeth, b. February 2, 1789, bapt. September 25, 1791. Spon: Parents.

Barbara, daughter of Joseph Kemmel and Elizabeth, b. February 1, 1791, bapt. September 25, 1791. Spon: Parents.

Dorothea, daughter of Henry Hinkel and Catharine, b. April 20, 1791, bapt. September 25, 1791. Spon: Dorothea Loscher, grandmother.

John, son of John Koerber and Maria Catharine, b. August 30, 1791, bapt. September 25, 1791. Spon: Parents.

William, son of Henry Froelich and Susanna Margaret, b. July 20, 1787, bapt. September 25, 1791. Spon: Parents.

Henry, son of Henry Froelich and Susanna Margaret, b. April 29, 1789, bapt. September 25, 1791. Spon: Parents.

Susanna, daughter of Henry Froelich and Susanna Margaret, b. July 22, 1791, bapt. September 25, 1791. Spon: Parents.

Margaret, daughter of George Herbel and Barbara, b. November 27, 1786, bapt. October 5, 1791. Spon: Parents.

Hannah, daughter of George Herbel and Barbara, b. July 11, 1789, bapt. October 5, 1791. Spon: Parents.

Henry, son of Jacob Weidman and Sarah, b. April 19, 1791, bapt. October 9, 1791. Spon: Parents.

Sarah, daughter of Henry Young and Elizabeth, b. May 23, 1790, bapt. October 16, 1791. Spon: Parents.

Isaac, son of John Rohrer and Margaret, b. August 14, 1791, bapt. October 16, 1791. Spon: Parents.

Maria, daughter of Jacob Gibler and Catharine, b. May 22, 1791, bapt. November 4, 1791. Spon: Parents.

William, son of David Noil and wife, b. July 25, 1791, bapt. November 6, 1791. Spon: Jacob Noeff and Anna.

Anna Gertrude, daughter of Peter Bockius and Rosina, b. October 5, 1786, bapt. November 20, 1791. Spon: Parents and Anna Gertrude Hess, grandmother.

Anna Elizabeth, daughter of Peter Bockius and Rosina, b. September

14, 1788, bapt. November 20, 1791. Spon: Parents, Anna Gertrude Hess, grandmother, and Anna Elizabeth Bockius.
Sarah, daughter of Joseph Bender and Catharine, b. June 6, 1876, bapt. November 20, 1791. Spon: Parents.
Francis, son of Joseph Bender and Catharine, b. February 6, 1788, bapt. November 20, 1791. Spon: Parents.
Catharine, daughter of William Stalman and Elizabeth, b. September 21, 1791, bapt. November 26, 1791. Spon: Julius Kerber and Catharine.
John Peter, son of John Peter Fuchs (Fusch) and Margaret, b. October 25, 1791, bapt. December 4, 1791. Spon: John Schlatter and Anna Magdalene.
Dorothea, daughter of Christopher Bockius and Sybilla (Sibylla), b. March 14, 1790, bapt. December 4, 1791. Spon: Elizabeth Bockius and Dorothea Lasch, grandmothers.
Christine, daughter of Christopher Bockius and Sibylla, b. November 27, 1791, bapt. December 4, 1791. Spon: Elizabeth Bockius and Dorothea Lasch, grandmothers.
John Henry, son of John Schuster and Elizabeth, b. Apirl 10, 1789, bapt. December 25, 1791. Spon: Henry Baehr and Margaret.
Charles, son of John Schuster and Elizabeth, b. October 7, 1791, bapt. ----, 1789. Spon: Parents.
Anna Charlotte, daughter of John Fred. Weinland and Charlotte, nee Fraes, b. December 23, 1791, bapt. December 27, 1791. Spon: Jacob Haegy and Anna Maria.

1792
Catharine, daughter of Jacob Umrath and Catharine, b. June 25, 1790, bapt. January 1, 1792. Spon: Parents.
Jacob, son of Jacob Staat and Barbara, b. May 27, 1782, bapt. January 1, 1792. Spon: Parents.
John, son of Jacob Staat and Barbara, b. October 28, 1784, bapt. January 1, 1792. Spon: Parents.
William, son of Jacob Staat and Barbara, b. April 30, 1788, bapt. January 1, 1792. Spon: Parents.
Maria, daughter of John Matthew Mueller and Elizabeth, b. January 10, 1787, bapt. January 11, 1792. Spon: Maria Leysinger.
John Matthew, son of John Matthew Mueller and Elizabeth, b. December 20, 1791, bapt. January 11, 1792. Spon: Parents.
John, son of Peter Schaurer and Catharine, b. May 8, 1791, bapt. January 15, 1792. Spon: Parents.
John, son of Daniel Synked and Dorothea, b. February 30, 1783, bapt. January 15, 1792. Spon: Parents.
Maria Margaret, daughter of Daniel Synked and Dorothea, b. May 17, 1789, bapt. January 15, 1792. Spon: Parents.
Samuel, son of Daniel Synked and Dorothea, b. December 10, 1791, bapt. January 15, 1792. Spon: Parents.
Justus, son of Jacob Staat and Barbara, b. January 11, 1792, bapt. February 10, 1792. Spon: Parents.
Benjamin, son of Michael Loewering and Catharine, b. October 31, 1790, bapt. February 17, 1792. Spon: Parents.
John, son of Michael Loewering and Catharine, b. November 1, 1791, bapt. February 17, 1792. Spon: Parents.
John, son of Andrew Riegler and Margaret, b. December 28, 1791, bapt. February 21, 1792. Spon: John Benner and Anna Maria.

Abraham, son of Henry Schermer and Maria, b. January 6, 1792, bapt. March 1, 1792. Spon: Abraham Koerber and Elizabeth.
Abraham, son of David Henrich and Maria, b. November 24, 1791, bapt. April 8, 1792. Spon: Parents.
John, son of John Haenz and Susanna, b. March 4, 1792, bapt. April 8, 1792. Spon: Parents.
Anthony, son of Henry Dewis and Maria, b. January 15, 1791, bapt. April 8, 1792. Spon: Parents.
Sarah Barbara, daughter of John Wenzel Karch and Maria, b. November 15, 1791, bapt. April 15, 1792. Spon: Christ. Haetzel and Barbara.
Maria Elizabeth, daughter of John Kerbach and Christine, b. December 10, 1791, bapt. April 15, 1792. Spon: Parents.
A child of ---- Wentzel and wife, b. ----, bapt. April 15, 1792. Spon: Philip Wentzel and wife, grandparents.
Jacob, son of John Schmidt and Elizabeth, b. April 17, 1792, bapt. May 6, 1792. Spon: Valentine Schmidt and Susanna.
Anna Elizabeth, daughter of Joseph Loebering and Anna Maria, b. May 21, 1792, bapt. May 6, 1792. Spon: Parents.
Daniel, son of George Schneider and Catharine, b. May 31, 1792, bapt. June 24, 1792. Spon: Parents.
Elizabeth, daughter of ---- Weil and wife, b. ----, bapt. June 10, 1792. Spon: Elizabeth Weil, of Philadelphia.
Anna, daughter of Jacob Henrich and Elizabeth, b. January 14, 1792, bapt. July 8, 1792. Spon: Parents.
Andrew, son of John Weil and Barbara, b. December 5, 1791, bapt. July 20, 1792. Spon: Parents.
Elizabeth, daughter of William Fuchs and Elizabeth Cath., b. October 4, 1791, bapt. July 20, 1792. Spon: Parents.
Anna Margaret, daughter of Peter Sterger and Elizabeth, b. May 6, 1792, bapt. July 22, 1792. Spon: Marg. Haupt, grandmother.
Martin, son of George Fleischhauer and Barbara, b. May 17, 1792, bapt. July 22, 1792. Spon: Martin Sommer and Elizabeth.
Magdalene, daughter of Abraham Paul and Barbara, b. May 5, 1791, bapt. August 6, 1792. Spon: Fred. Schmidt and wife.
Esther, daughter of John Schmidt and Elizabeth, b. February 13, 1789, bapt. May --, 1789. Spon: Parents.
George, son of John Staudt and Maria, b. January 23, 1792, bapt. August 17, 1792. Spon: The father.
Regina Rachel, daughter of George Benner and Magdalene, b. April 26, 1776, bapt. August 21, 1792. Spon: Parents.
Rebecca, daughter of John Wentzel and Elizabeth, b. July 1, 1792, bapt. August 26, 1792. Spon: Francis Wentzel and Christine, grandparents.
Sophia, daughter of John Landenberger and Anna Maria, b. March 27, 1792, bapt. August 26, 1792. Spon: Sophia Kraemer.
Jacob, son of Jacob Parall and Dorothea, b. August 25, 1792, bapt. September 3, 1792. Spon: Parents.
A child of Henry Thiel and wife of Philadelphia, b. ----, bapt. August 26, 1792, at Frankfort. Spon: Parents.
Maria Catharine, daughter of Godfrey Bockius and Eva, b. August 21, 1792, bapt. September 10, 1792. Spon: Ludwig Wolf and Maria.
Sarah, daughter of Jacob Sorber and Anna, b. March 5, 1790, bapt. September 11, 1792. Spon: Parents.
Magdalene, daughter of Jacob Sorber and Anna, b. June 4, 1792,

bapt. September 11, 1792. Spon: Parents.

Elizabeth Maria, daughter of John Jacob Dieter and Eva Christine, b. March 15, 1786, bapt. September 18, 1792. Spon: Elizabeth Maria Schlatter, grandmother.

Maria Magdalena, daughter of Henry Weissbrod and Maria, b. September 1, 1792, bapt. September 23, 1792. Spon: Maria Magd. Dauenheimer and Baltzer Hertzog.

John, son of Jacob Oberdorff and Maria, b. September 19, 1792, bapt. October 17, 1792. Spon: Parents.

John, son of Peter Weidner and Susanna, b. June 21, 1791, bapt. October 17, 1792. Spon: The Father.

Joseph, son of Joseph Sorber anad wife, b. October 15, 1792, bapt. October 21, 1792. Spon: Parents.

Henry, son of Henry Rohrer and Elizabeth, b. December 1, 1791, bapt. October 21, 1792. Spon: Parents.

Henry, son of Henry Schoch and Sarah, b. October 20, 1792, bapt. October 21, 1792. Spon: Michael Schoch and Margaret.

Barbara, daughter of Jacob Remy and Anna, b. July 21, 1791, bapt. November 12, 1792. Spon: Parents.

Lawrence, son of Jacob Remy and Anna, b. August 6, 1792, bapt. November 12, 1792. Spon: Parents.

Carl Giebler, son of Frederick Herman, p.l., and Maria, b. October 24, 1792, bapt. November 21, 1792. Spon: Godfrey Giebler and Catharine, wife, of Philadelphia.

William, son of Christopher Ottinger and Anna, b. July 4, 1792, bapt. November 25, 1792. Spon: Henry Meyer and Catharine.

Redman, son of Thomas Oinz and Margaret, b. October 24, 1792, bapt. December 6, 1792. Spon: Parents.

Elizabeth, daughter of Casper Meyer and Maria, b. October 13, 1792, bapt. December 23, 1792. Spon: Parents.

John George, son of John Koerber and Maria Catharine, b. November 17, 1792, bapt. December 30, 1792. Spon: Julius Koerber and Catharine.

Anna, daughter of Anthony Zander and Margaret, b. December 19, 1788, bapt. December 30, 1792. Spon: Parents.

Maria Eva, daughter of Anthony Zander and Margaret, b. February 23, 1791, bapt. December 30, 1792. Spon: Parents.

Samuel, son of William Dasten and Barbara, b. March 7, 1790, bapt. December 30, 1792. Spon: Parents.

1793

Robert, son of James Orr and Margaret, b. May 22, 1790, bapt. January 8, 1793. Spon: Parents.

William, son of James Orr and Margaret, b. June 27, 1792, bapt. January 8, 1793. Spon: Parents.

Jacob, son of Henry Schnabel and Veronica, b. October 19, 1792, bapt. January 20, 1793. Spon: Parents.

William, son of Henry Gyhly and Elizabeth, b. January 10, 1792, bapt. February --, 1793. Spon: Adam Schneider and wife.

Joseph, son of George Leonhard and Christine, b. January 31, 1788, bapt. ----. Spon: Parents.

Christine, daughter of George Leonhard and Christine, b. March 10, 1792, bapt. February --, 1793. Spon: Parents.

Maria, daughter of Peter de Dieuv and Maria Eva, b. October 7, 1792, bapt. February --, 1793. Spon: Parents.

Albert, son of Peter Bockius and Rosina, b. June 26, 1792, bapt. February 26, 1793. Spon: Parents.
Maria, daughter of Leonard Maertz and Anna, b. December 19, 1792, bapt. March 3, 1793. Spon: Anna Goettinger.
Henry, son of Henry Schutz, Jr. and wife, b. October 24, 1792, bapt. March 18, 1793. Spon: Parents.
William, son of George Bressler and Maria, b. November 12, 1792, bapt. March 17, 1793. Spon: Parents.
John, son of Jacob Miller and Mary Magdalene, b. January 29, 1793, bapt. April 2, 1793. Spon: Parents.
George, son of Rudolph Krauer and Elizabeth, b. October 29, 1792, bapt. April 7, 1793. Spon: Ludwig Krauer and Margaret.
Margaret, daughter of Philip Schinkel and Catharine, b. November 26, 1792, bapt. April 7, 1793. Spon: ---- Dickhaud and wife Anna.
Martin, son of Alexander Lassey and Anna, b. January 25, 1793, bapt. April 7, 1793. Spon: The Mother.
Mariana, daughter of George Styhl and Elizabeth, b. September 6, 1789, bapt. April 14, 1793. Spon: Parents.
John, son of George Styhl and Elizabeth, b. December 2, 1791, bapt. April 14, 1793. Spon: Parents.
Frederick, son of Jacob Emrich and Elizabeth, b. March 13, 1793, bapt. April 14, 1793. Spon: Frederick Emrich, grandfather.
Margaret, daughter of Jacob Meyer and Margaret, b. March 14, 1793, bapt. April 14, 1793. Spon: Parents and grandparents.
Elizabeth, daughter of John Meyer and Anna, b. February 18, 1793, bapt. April 14, 1793. Spon: Parents and grandparents.
Valentine, son of Valentine Koerber and Margaret, b. April 17, 1793, bapt. April 18, 1793. Spon: Parents.
John, son of William Staudt and Margaret, b. January 16, 1793, bapt. May 8, 1793. Spon: Parents.
Andrew, son of Peter Blaecker and Hannah, b. January 4, 1793, bapt. May 19, 1793. Spon: Andrew Berner and Elizabeth.
Maria, daughter of James Brown and Anna, b. March 31, 1791, bapt. May 26, 1793. Spon: Parents.
John George, son of John Drong and Sarah, b. November 9, 1792, bapt. June 16, 1793. Spon: George Braun and Maria.
A child of Christoph Ottinger and Anna, b. May 4, 1793, bapt. June 19, 1793. Spon: Henry Mayer and Catharine.
Elizabeth, daughter of N. Grosskopf and Anna Margaret, b. July 25, 1788, bapt. July 24, 1793. Spon: Valentine Koenig and Anna Margaret.
Charles, son of Philip Fischer and Maria, b. July 19, 1792, bapt. July 24, 1793. Spon: Parents.
August, son of Peter Umrighaus and Maria, b. ----, bapt. ----, 1793. Spon: Parents.
Francis, son of Peter Thiel and wife, b. February 11, 1792, bapt. July 2, 1793. Spon: Parents.
John, son of John Pecky and Barbara, b. September 28, 1791, bapt. July 8, 1793. Spon: Parents.
Petrus, son of Rudolph Froely and Elizabeth, b. September 25, 1792, bapt. July 14, 1793. Spon: Parents.
Dorothea, daughter of Conrad Lens and Marg., b. February 27, 1792, bapt. July 18, 1793. Spon: Parents.
John, son of Anthony Bicony and wife, b. May 13, 1793, bapt. July

24, 1793. Spon: Parents.
Elizabeth, daughter of Christoph Ossius and Elizabeth, b. June 26, 1793, bapt. July 24, 1793. Spon: Parents.
David, son of John Rohrer and Margaret, b. June 17, 1793, bapt. July 20, 1793. Spon: Parents.
William, son of Peter Scheurer and Catharine, b. ----, bapt. August 1, 1793. Spon: Parents.
Bernard, son of Bernard Bockius and Barbara Gress, b. March 3, 1792, bapt. September 2, 1793. Spon: John Hettebach and Maria.
William, son of Jacob Grosskopf and Elizabeth, b. January 13, 1793, bapt. September --, 1793. Spon: Parents.
John, son of John Sorber and wife, b. August 8, 1793, bapt. September 23, 1793. Spon: Parents.
Catharine, daughter of Justus Schultz and wife, b. July 1, 1793, bapt. September 23, 1793. Spon: Parents.
Anna, daughter of Werner Dewald and Mary Magdalene, b. June 1, 1793, bapt. September 23, 1793. Spon: Parents.
Maria Elizabeth, daughter of Christian Vetter and Annette Catharine, b. August 21, 1793, bapt. September 29, 1793. Spon: John Jacob Schlatter and the grandmother.
Elizabeth, daughter of John Schmidt and Elizabeth, b. December 8, 1792, bapt. October 6, 1793. Spon: Parents.
A child of George Schuster and wife, b. ----, bapt. October 13, 1793. Spon: J. Hetzel and wife.
Rebecca, daughter of Frederick Younker and Anna Barbara, b. August 18, 1791, bapt. ----, 1793. Spon: Henry Sorber and Catharine.
Anna Barbara, daughter of Henry Sorber and Catharine, b. May 27, 1793, bapt. ----, 1793. Spon: Frederick Yunker and Anna Barbara.
Ludwig, son of Ludwig Guilliams and Elizabeth, b. October 11, 1793, bapt. October 18, 1793. Spon: The father.
Susanna, daughter of Joseph Biconet and Anna, b. September 20, 1793, bapt. October 27, 1793. Spon: Pater (the father) and Miss Ecky from Philadelphia.
Henry, son of Christoph Wunter and Anna, b. October 20, 1792, bapt. November 3, 1793. Spon: Henry Schweyer and wife.
Elizabeth, daughter of John Dutweiler and Barbara, b. January 14, 1793, bapt. November 16, 1793. Spon: Parents.
Margaret, daughter of Rewo Stivens and Margaret, b. October 5, 1793, bapt. November 21, 1793. Spon: Parents.
Hannah, daughter of Henry Schermer and Maria, b. October 27, 1793, bapt. December 26, 1793. Spon: Abraham Schermer and Maria Koerber.
Jacob, son of Jacob Henrich and Elizabeth, b. October 13, 1793, bapt. December 26, 1793. Spon: Parents and Maria Ens.

1794
Susanna, daughter of David Henrich and Dorothea, b. April 3, 1793, bapt. January --, 1794. Spon: Parents.
Sarah, daughter of Henry Duttweiler and Sarah, b. April 25, 1793, bapt. ----, 1794. Spon: Philip Schwartz and Susanna.
Ann Margaret, daughter of Richard Warren and Catharine, b. August 4, 1793, bapt. January 12, 1794. Spon: Parents.
Thomas, son of Edward Jefferts and Barbara, b. December 15, 1793, bapt. February 2, 1794. Spon: Parents.

Sally, daughter of Jacob Grensebach and Christine, b. September 30, 1793, bapt. February 2, 1794. Spon: Parents.
Anna Elizabeth, daughter of John Schuster and Elizabeth, b. January 2, 1794, bapt. March 2, 1794. Spon: George Schmidt and Elizabeth.
Samuel, son of Henry Behr and Magdalene, b. November 3, 1793, bapt. March 2, 1794. Spon: Parents.
Anna Barbara, daughter of John Haentz and Susanna, b. February 15, 1794, bapt. March 30, 1794. Spon: Peter Haentz and Anna Barbara Will.
Daniel, son of Michael Kayser and Catharine, b. March 28, 1793, bapt. April 11, 1794. Spon: Gertrude Hess, grandmother.

Children of Anthony Gilbert and Elizabeth, nee Nutz:
Margaret, b. April 1, 1774.
Samuel, b. December 5, 1775.
Charles, b. April 22, 1778.
Elizabeth, b. November 14, 1780.
Leonard, b. June 15, 1783.
Sarah, b. January 14, 1785.
August, b. August 10, 1788.
Juliana, b. July 2, 1791.
The above children were baptized April 13, 1794. The sponsors were the parents and Leonard Nutz and wife Margaret.

John Jacob, son of Adam Schlatter and Maria, b. February 16, 1794, bapt. April 18, 1794. Spon: John Jacob Schlatter and Anna Cath. Althaus.
Charles, son of Stephen Singlewoud and Anna, b. September 27, 1793, bapt. July 29, 1794. Spon: Parents.
Magdalene, daughter of Jacob Geissel and wife, b. July 15, 1793, bapt. May --, 1794. Spon: Parents.
Daniel, son of Jacob Weidman and wife, b. ----, bapt. May --, 1794. Spon: Christian Geissel and wife.
Elizabeth, daughter of Henry Gerster and Anna, b. December 1, 1793, bapt. May --, 1794. Spon: Parents.
Elizabeth, daughter of Daniel Beltz and Susanna, b. May 1, 1793, bapt. May --, 1794. Spon: Parents.
A child of Henry Rohrer and Barbara, b. September 15, 1792, bapt. May --, 1794. Spon: Parents.
Elizabeth, daughter of Joseph Rohrer and Catharine, b. March 1, 1794, bapt. May --, 1794. Spon: Parents.
Anna Catharine, daughter of John Jacob Dieter and Eva Christine, b. June 12, 1793, bapt. June 8, 1794. Spon: Mrs. Schlatter, grandmother.
Anna Catharine, daughter of Adam Schlatter and Maria Catharine, b. October 8, 1795, bapt. ----, 1795. Spon: Christian Vetter and Annette Cath.
Regina, daughter of John Gartner and Catharine, b. May 1, 1794, bapt. June 27, 1794. Spon: J. Gartner and wife, Grandparents.
James, son of James Brown and Anna, b. January 14, 1794, bapt. June 27, 1794. Spon: Parents.
Jacob, son of David Merckel and Susanna, b. April 25, 1794, bapt. June 29, 1794. Spon: Parents.
Thomas, son of John Oblecker and Barbara, b. June 27, 1794, bapt.

July 26, 1794. Spon: Parents.

Edmond Randolph, son of Frederick Herman, p.l., and Maria, b. July 13, 1794, bapt. August 3, 1794. Spon: Parents.

Anna Maria, daughter of John Fromberger and wife, b. August 19, 1793, bapt. August 17, 1794. Spon: John Fromberger and Anna Maria, Grandparents.

William, son of Michael Kehrbach and Catharine, b. April 6, 1794, bapt. August 17, 1794. Spon: Parents.

Esther, daughter of Wendel Karg and Maria, b. November 12, 1793, bapt. August 17, 1794. Spon: Parents.

Anna Maria, daughter of John Landenberger and Anna Maria, b. September 22, 1793, bapt. August 17, 1794. Spon: Parents.

Catharine Margaret, daughter of George Jacob and Christine, b. June 25, 1794, bapt. August 31, 1794. Spon: Philip Jacob and Cath. Margaret.

Anna, daughter of Jacob Koerber and Elizabeth, b. April 24, 1794, bapt. September 11, 1794. Spon: Parents.

Margaret Charlotte, daughter of John Peter Irlenhauser and Anna Margaret, b. August 18, 1794, bapt. November 27, 1794. Spon: Charlotte Eichbaum and Margaret Roth.

John Philip, son of John Henry Weissbrod and Maria, b. October 18, 1794, bapt. ----, 1794. Spon: The Grandparents.

Catharine Elizabeth, daughter of John Landenberger and Anna Maria, b. July 30, 1787, bapt. ----, 1794. Spon: Parents.

George and William, sons of John Landenberger and Anna Maria, b. March 21, 1789, bapt. ----, 1794. Spon: Parents.

George, son of George Jacob Kuehle and Maria Dorothea, b. November 20, 1769, bapt. ----. Spon: Parents.

John, son of George Jacob Kuehle and Maria Dorothea, b. December 19, 1783, bapt. ----. Spon: Parents.

Elizabeth, daughter of George Jacob Kuehle and Maria Dorothea, b. April 15, 1779, bapt. ----. Spon: Parents.

1795

Margaret, daughter of George Leonhard and Christine, b. June 3, 1795(1794?), bapt. January 26, 1795. Spon: Parents.

John, son of Jacob Baralle and Dorothy, b. December 3, 1794, bapt. February 1, 1795. Spon: The Grandparents.

George, son of John Haentz and Anna Regina, b. November 9, 1794, bapt. February 1, 1795. Spon: Parents.

John, son of John Hammelbach and Maria Susanna, b. March 1, 1790, bapt. February 1, 1794. Spon: Parents.

Peter, son of Lawrence Trong and wife, b. November 18, 1793, bapt. February 1, 1795. Spon: Parents.

Adam, son of Lawrence Trong and wife, b. December 7, ----, bapt. February 8, 1795. Spon: Parents.

Sally, daughter of William Dosten and Barbara, b. December 24, 1794, bapt. February 23, 1795. Spon: Parents.

Anna, daughter of Henry Schuetz and Elizabeth, b. December 20, 1794, bapt. February 26, 1795. Spon: Parents.

Veronica, daughter of Philip Riffert and Ursilla, b. December 16, 1794, bapt. February 26, 1795. Spon: Parents.

Margaret, daughter of Michael Lange and Margaret, b. January 5, 1795, bapt. February 28, 1795. Spon: Parents.

Children of Peter Streber and Ernestina, baptized November 9, 1794:
Peter, son of Peter Streber and Ernestina, b. September 20, 1794.
Catharine, daughter of Peter Streber and Ernestina, b. June 24, 1789.
Bernard, son of Peter Streber and Ernestina, b. March 14, 1787.
Daniel, son of Peter Streber and Ernestina, b. August 29, 1784.
Leonard, son of Peter Streber and Ernestina, b. June 21, 1780.
Mary, daughter of Peter Streber and Ernestina, b. April 9, 1782.
Rebecca, daughter of Peter Streber and Ernestina, b. November 17, 1791.
The parents were the sponsors.

Margaret, daughter of George Bressler and Maria Catharine, b. February 18, 1795, bapt. March 29, 1795. Spon: ----.
Samuel, son of Samuel Gaebler and Maria Keli (Kelly), b. November 13, 1794, bapt. ----, 1795. Spon: Parents.
Jacob, son of John Barrett and wife, b. March 25, 1795, bapt. April 19, 1795. Spon: Parents.
Polly, daughter of ---- Hinkel and wife, b. February 20, 1794, bapt. April 19, 1795. Spon: Parents.
Samuel, daughter of Peter Deal and wife, b. January 11, 1791, bapt. ----. Spon: Parents.
Sarah, daughter of Abraham Schermer and Christine, b. November 28, 1794, bapt. May 17, 1795. Spon: Jacob Grosskopf and Elizabeth.
Sarah, daughter of John Kerber and Maria Catharine, b. November 24, 1794, bapt. May 25, 1795. Spon: The Mother.
Francis, son of Richard Hikam and Magdalene, b. December 12, 1792, bapt. May 29, 1795. Spon: Parents.
Anna Catharine, daughter of Richard Hikam and Magdalene, b. September 1, 1794, bapt. May 29, 1795. Spon: Henry Folck and Anna Catharine.
Henry, son of Henry Folck and Anna Catharine, b. July 10, 1791, bapt. ----, 1795. Spon: Parents.
Andrew, son of Henry Folck and Anna Catharine, b. July 3, 1792, bapt. ----, 1795. Spon: Parents.
John Henry, son of Bernard Schuckert and Maria, b. June 27, 1793, bapt. ----, 1795. Spon: Parents.
John Jacob, son of Henry Sorber and wife, b. August 16, 1794, bapt. ----, 1795. Spon: Jacob Sorber.
Sarah, daughter of Jacob Miller and Susanna, b. July 15, 1787, bapt. ----, 1795. Spon: Parents.
James Derre, son of Peter Worrell and Margaret, b. April 25, 1794, bapt. ----, 1795. Spon: Parents.
George Philip, son of John Wenzel and Elizabeth, b. April 17, 1793, bapt. July 5, 1795. Spon: Parents.
John Week, son of John Fromberger and wife, b. January 18, 1795, bapt. July 5, 1795. Spon: The Grandparents.
John, son of Andrew Warner and Dorothy, b. August 15, 1794, bapt. July 5, 1795. Spon: Parents.
Margaret, daughter of Samuel Deal and Elizabeth Kampman, b. January 4, 1795, bapt. July 5, 1795. Spon: Parents.
Elizabeth, daughter of John Landenberger and wife Anna Maria, b. April 18, 1795, bapt. July 9, 1795. Spon: Parents.
Hannah, daughter of Anthony Bigony and wife, b. January 27, 1795, bapt. July 9, 1795. Spon: Parents.

Peter, son of John Mann and Elizabeth, b. July 17, 1795, bapt. July 29, 1795. Spon: Peter Mann and Elizabeth, Grandparents.

Children of George Miller and Mary Magdalene, baptized July 30, 1795:
Margaret, b. June 29, 1790.
John George, b. February 14, 1785.
Rachel, b. May 26, 1786.
Philip, b. December 25, 1787.
Maria, b. February 4, 1789.
William, b. December 2, 1794.
John, b. August 13, 1795.
The parents were the sponsors.

Susanna, daughter of Michael Loebering and Catharine, b. February 29, 1794, bapt. July 9, 1795. Spon: Parents.
Margaret, daughter of Peter Weidner and Susanna, b. February 17, 1794, bapt. July 9, 1795. Spon: Parents.
Joseph, son of Joseph Loebering and Anna Maria, b. January 9, 1795, bapt. July 9, 1795. Spon: Parents.
John, son of Henry Schnabel and Veronica, b. March 28, 1795, bapt. July 22, 1795. Spon: Parents.
Henry George, son of Justus Schuetz and Catharine, b. August 5, 1795, bapt. September 3, 1795. Spon: Parents and Mrs. Scheutz, grandmother.
Anna, daughter of Jacob Murer and Esther, b. December 1, 1794, bapt. September 10, 1795. Spon: Parents.
Elizabeth, daughter of William Staut and Margaret, b. August 29, 1794, bapt. November 9, 1795. Spon: Parents.
Conrad, son of Conrad Ax and Maria, b. November 15, 1795, bapt. December 6, 1795. Spon: Henry Fischer and Margaret.
Sarah, daughter of N. Croniker and wife, b. October 14, 1795, bapt. December 6, 1795. Spon: Joseph Staudt and Rosina.
Catharine, daughter of Daniel Beltz and wife, b. November 27, 1795, bapt. December 20, 1795. Spon: Jacob Steinmeier and Catharine.
Elizabeth, daughter of Philip Schinkel and wife, b. April 22, 1795, bapt. ----, 1795. Spon: N. Schaeffer and wife.
Elizabeth, daughter of Michael Kerbach and Catharine, b. June 27, 1795, bapt. ----, 1795. Spon: Parents.
Isabella, daughter of Robert Thomson and Esther, b. November 24, 1795, bapt. ----, 1795. Spon: Parents.
John, son of Davis Shettinger and Maria, b. November 8, 1795, bapt. ----, 1795. Spon: The Mother.

1796
Sarah, daughter of John Dutweiler and Barbara, b. September 11, 1795, bapt. January 10, 1796. Spon: Parents.
John, son of Peter Blecker and wife, b. ----, 1795, bapt. January 10, 1796. Spon: Andrew Berner and wife.
Peter, son of George Miller and Mary Magdalene, b. January 1, 1796, bapt. February 8, 1796. Spon: Parents.
Anna, daughter of Frederick Junker and Barbara, b. November 27, 1793, bapt. February 30, 1796(?). Spon: Anna Sorber, grandmother.
Elizabeth, daughter of Frederick Voeckel and Anna Elizabeth, b. May

2, 1791, bapt. May 6, 1796. Spon: Ludwig Hans and Parents.
Ludwig, son of Frederick Voelkel and Anna Elizabeth, b. March 2, 1795, bapt. May 6, 1796. Spon: Ludwig Hans and Parents.
Anna, daughter of David Merckel and Susanna, b. December 11, 1795, bapt. February --, 1796. Spon: Parents.
David, son of Jacob Karg and Anna, b. May 23, 1791, bapt. May 25, 1796. Spon: The Mother.
Jacob, son of Joseph Sorber and Elizabeth, b. October 24, 1793, bapt. March 25, 1796. Spon: Parents.
Sarah, daughter of Daniel Haeagy and Mary Magdalene, b. May 29, 1795, bapt. March 27, 1796. Spon: Parents.
Maria, daughter of John Rohrer and Margaret, b. February 11, 1796, bapt. March 27, 1796. Spon: Frederick Herman and Maria.
Daniel, son of Joseph Rohrer and wife, b. October 14, 1795, bapt. March 27, 1796. Spon: Parents.
John, son of John Hommer and Catharine, b. October 2, 1796(1795?), bapt. April 3, 1796. Spon: Parents.
Hannah, daughter of Michael Haas and Anna Maria, b. June 16, 1785, bapt. April 3, 1796. Spon: Philip Weber and Anna, grandparents.
Anna Maria, daughter of Michael Haas and Anna Maria, b. April 9, 1789, bapt. April 3, 1796. Spon: Philip Weber and Anna, grandparents.
Maria, daughter of Michael Haas and Anna Maria, b. November 25, 1792, bapt. April 3, 1796. Spon: Philip Weber and Anna, grandparents.
Jacob, son of ---- Staudt and wife, b. ----, bapt. September 26, 1796. Spon: ----.
John, son of Robert Bauman and Salome, b. October 22, 1795, bapt. May 29, 1796. Spon: Parents.
John, son of James Brown and Anna, b. April 28, 1796, bapt. May 29, 1796. Spon: Parents.
Samuel, son of William Hagy and Catharine, b. June 11, 1795, bapt. June --, 1796. Spon: Samuel Friess and wife.
A. F. Frederick, son of Frederick Herman, pastor loci, and Maria, b. June 10, 1796, bapt. July 2, 1796. Spon: Parents.
Ellis, son of George Kiel and Catharine, b. April 19, 1795, bapt. August 21, 1796. Spon: Parents.
Esther, daughter of Christopher Bockius and Elizabeth, b. October 11, 1795, bapt. September 1, 1796. Spon: The Mother and grandmother.
George, son of George Clauss and Margaret Dorothy, b. September 25, 1795, bapt. September 2, 1796. Spon: Parents.
Anna, daughter of David Niwill and Anna, b. October 6, 1783, bapt. September 11, 1796. Spon: Parents.
Nelly, daughter of David Niwill and Anna, b. September 26, 1796 (1795?), bapt. September 11, 1796. Spon: Parents.
Jacob, son of Jacob Neff and Polly, b. November 12, 1795, bapt. September 11, 1796. Spon: Parents.
Alexander, son of Robert Davison and Esther, b. June 30, 1796, bapt. September 11, 1796. Spon: Parents.
Susanna, daughter of Christ. Gutknecht and Elizabeth, b. November 24, 1795, bapt. October 4, 1796. Spon: Parents.
Hannah, daughter of John Mayer and wife, b. September 19, 1796, bapt. October 9, 1796. Spon: ----.

Sarah, daughter of George Bressler and Anna Catharine, b. September 26, 1796, bapt. October 9, 1796. Spon: Parents.
John Frederick, son of John Krafft Schneider and Maria Elizabeth, b. September 29, 1796, bapt. October 9, 1796. Spon: Jacob Jung, Fred. Henrich and Cath. Pratt.
Sally, daughter of Archibald McCan and Catharine, b. March 2, 1794, bapt. October 10, 1796. Spon: Parents.
Archibald, son of Archibald McCan and Catharine, b. September 20, 1796, bapt. October 10, 1796. Spon: Parents.
Henry, son of George Jacob and Christine, b. March 4, 1796, bapt. October 16, 1796. Spon: Henry Oberlaender and wife.
Joseph, son of Jacob Schlatter and Elizabeth, b. October 27, 1796, bapt. December 5, 1796. Spon: Parents.
George Simon, son of George Hink, Jr. and Christine, b. September 29, 1796, bapt. November 15, 1796. Spon: George Wm. Fiebeck and Marg. Thiel.
Jonathan Lusley of Frankfort, 23 years old, b. ----, bapt. November --, 1796. Spon: ----.
John, son of Jonathan Lusley and Barbara, b. September 19, 1796, bapt. November --, 1796. Spon: Parents.
A child of John Salter and wife, b. ----, bapt. December -- 1796. Spon: ----.
Elizabeth, daughter of William Hottenstein and Elizabeth, b. November 13, 1797(?), bapt. December 25, 1796. Spon: Christ. Gutknecht and Elizabeth.
Esther, daughter of ---- Kerper and wife, b. April 9, 1796, bapt. December 25, 1796. Spon: Parents.
Deborah, daughter of Jacob Geissler and Hannah, b. December 15, 1795, bapt. December 25, 1796. Spon: Parents.
Maria, daughter of Godfrey Bockius and Sally, b. September 12, 1796, bapt. December 28, 1796. Spon: Parents.

1797
Anthony, son of Christian Haentz and Catharine, b. February 21, 1797[?], bapt. January 11, 1797. Spon: Christ. Wetting and Elette.
Francis William, son of Francis Bockius and Susanna, b. July 16, 1794, bapt. ----, 1796. Spon: Parents.
Henry, son of ---- Kerper and wife, b. October 27, 1796, bapt. January 8, 1797. Spon: Parents.
Samuel, son of Henry Froely and Susanna, b. ----, 1796, bapt. January 20, 1797. Spon: Parents.
Francisca, of Henry Froely and Susanna, b. ----, bapt. January 20, 1797. Spon: Parents.
William, son of Samuel McFerran and Hannah, b. September 13, 1797 (1796), bapt. January 12, 1797. Spon: Parents.
Samuel, son of Peter Schaurer and Catharine, b. August 21, 1796, bapt. January 21, 1797. Spon: Parents.
George, son of Jacob Gibler and Catharine, b. July 30, 1796, bapt. January 25, 1797. Spon: Parents.
John Daniel, son of Conrad Ax and wife, b. January 7, 1797, bapt. January 25, 1797. Spon: John Daniel Beltz and wife.
John, son of John Schlatter and Anna Magdalene, b. December 17, 1796, bapt. February 2, 1797. Spon: John Stein and Magdalene.
Peter, son of William Staudt and Margaret, b. March 8, 1796, bapt.

January 4, 1797. Spon: Parents.

Children of Charles Ristlein and Hannah, bapt. February 5, 1797:
Elizabeth, b. April 1, 1783.
Joseph, b. July 4, 1785.
Catharine, b. March 11, 1788.
John, b. September 25, 1790.
Charles, b. August 31, 1793.
Anna, b. July 12, 1796.

Daniel, son of John Kerbach and Christine, b. December 7, 1796, bapt. February 5, 1797. Spon: Daniel Kerbach and Rosina.
William, son of Jacob Weidman and wife, b. December 10, 1796, bapt. February 14, 1797. Spon: Parents.
Elizabeth, daughter of Adam Hausholter and Christine, b. November 8, 1796, bapt. February 26, 1797. Spon: Parents.
Elizabeth, daughter of Paul van Acken and wife, b. January 3, 1797, bapt. February 26, 1797. Spon: Parents.
Peter, son of Michael Lange and Margaret, b. October 20, 1796, bapt. March 19, 1797. Spon: Parents.
Daniel, son of Daniel Schmidt and Miriam, b. November 25, 1796, bapt. April 29, 1797. Spon: Parents.
Elizabeth, daughter of Abraham Seltzer and Margaret, b. January 13, 1797, bapt. April 7, 1797. Spon: George Krueger and Elizabeth Kureger.
Joseph, son of John Haentz and Susanna, b. August 16, 1795, bapt. July 16, 1797. Spon: Parents.
John George, son of John Haentz and Susanna, b. April 23, 1797, bapt. July 16, 1797. Spon: Parents.
Samuel Miller, son of (Peter) Worrel and wife, b. ----, bapt. July 15, 1797. Spon: Parents.
Anna Maria, daughter of Henry Leer and Anna Catharine, b. December 12, 1795, bapt. July 17, 1797. Spon: Peter Ohlwein and Parents.
John Peter, son of Henry Leer and Anna Catharine, b. December 21, 1796, bapt. July 17, 1797. Spon: Peter Ohlwein and Parents.
Catharine, daughter of Christopher Ossius and wife, b. March 11, 1797, bapt. ----, 1797. Spon: Parents.
Deborah, daughter of Michael Loevering and Catharine, b. September 11, 1797, bapt. ----, 1797. Spon: Parents.
Joseph, son of Joseph Bygony and wife, b. February 20, 1797, bapt. ----, 1797. Spon: Parents.
Maria, daughter of Godfrey Bockius and wife, b. September 12, 1797, bapt. ----, 1797. Spon: Parents.
Edward, son of Etienne Dutilh and Catharine Magdalene, b. July 22, 1797, bapt. October 10, 1797. Spon: Parents and Henriette Elizab. Nothnagel for Cath., Martin Widmer.
John Paul, son of John Adam Schlatter and Maria Catharine, b. August 11, 1797, bapt. October 14, 1797. Spon: John Paul Schlatter and Anna Magdalene.
John, son of Joseph Goodwin and Elizabeth, b. October 30, 1796, bapt. October 14, 1797. Spon: Parents.
Samuel, son of ---- Benner and wife, b. July 23, 1793, bapt. October --, 1797. Spon: Parents.
Elizabeth, daughter of ---- Benner and wife, b. September 6, 1795,

bapt. October --, 1797. Spon: Parents.
Martin, son of ---- Benner and wife, b. June 16, 1797, bapt. October --, 1797. Spon: Parents.
James, son of Jacob Rehl and Susanna, b. September 1, 1797, bapt. ----, 1797. Spon: Parents.
John, son of Philip Braun and Catharine, b. June 22, 1797, bapt. ----. Spon: Parents.
Elizabeth, daughter of Richard Hickson and Elizabeth, b. May 27, 1797, bapt. ----. Spon: Parents.

1798
Elizabeth, daughter of Philip Fischer and Maria, b. November 5, 1797, bapt. January 1, 1798. Spon: Parents.
Jacob Reimy, son of Jacob Reimy and Anna, b. in Frankfort on June 21, 1770, bapt. ----. Spon: ----.
Jacob, son of Jacob Reimy and Anna, b. November 9, 1797, bapt. ---. Spon: Parents.

Children of George Leonhard and Christine, bapt. 1798:
John, b. May 28, 1778.
George, b. September 26, 1779.
Jonathan, b. December 31, 1780.
Anna Maria, b. August 25, 1784.
Henry, b. November 22, 1785.
Joseph, b. January 30, 1788.
Christian, b. March 10, 1792.

Susanna, daughter of John Schmidt and Elizabeth, b. February 10, 1798, bapt. ----, 1798. Spon: Parents.
Elizabeth, daughter of Peter Streber and Ernestina, b. February 10, 1797, bapt. January 10, 1798. Spon: Parents.
Samuel, son of Peter Haentz and Elizabeth, b. December 25, 1798, bapt. ----, 1798. Spon: Parents.

Children of George Schuester and Barbara:
Jacob, son of George Schuster and Barbara, b. October 30, 1798.
George, son of George Schuster and Barbara, b. August 16, 1787.
John, son of George Schuster and Barbara, b. March 16, 1789.
Barbara, daughter of George Schuster and Barbara, b. December 22, 1790.
William, son of George Schuster and Barbara, b. May 12, 1797.
Sponsors were the parents and the grandfather.

Children of William Stevenson and Eleonora, bapt. February 12, 1798:
Francisca, b. February 17, 1787.
John, b. January 31, 1789.
William, b. March 23, 1792.
Thomas, b. August 2, 1795.
Sponsors: The parents.

Margaret (Peggy), daughter of Henry Mayer and Margaret, b. December 31, 1782, bapt. April 2, 1798. Spon: Parents.
Jacob, son of Henry Mayer and Margaret, b. September 3, 1785, bapt. April 2, 1798. Spon: Parents.

George, son of Henry Sorber and Catharine, b. April 16, 1797, bapt. May --, 1798. Spon: ----.
Anna, daughter of Robert Thomson and Esther, b. January 8, 1798, bapt. May --, 1798. Spon: Parents.
Maria Elizabeth, daughter of Bernard Schucherd and Maria, b. January 28, 1796, bapt. June --, 1798. Spon: Parents.
Anna Margaret, daughter of Bernard Schucherd and Maria, b. February 26, 1798, bapt. June --, 1798. Spon: Parents.
Edmunia Theresa, daughter of Fredk. Herman, p.l., and Mary, b. May 8, 1798, bapt. May 18, 1798. Spon: Parents.
Mary, daughter of George Abel and Dorothea, b. September 10, 1798, bapt. October 15, 1798. Spon: Parents.
Anna Louisa, daughter of George William Steinhauer and Catharine, b. July 21, 1798, bapt. ----, 1798. Spon: Parents.
David, son of David Rorman and wife, b. February 26, 1795, bapt. July 16, 1798. Spon: The Father.
Christian, son of John Pettely and Elizabeth, b. November 27, 1795, bapt. July 16, 1798. Spon: Parents.
Anna Maria, daughter of John Pettely and Elizabeth, b. October 9, 1797, bapt. July 16, 1798. Spon: Parents.
John, son of John Kreiter and Anna Dorothea, b. April 26, 1794, bapt. July 16, 1798. Spon: Parents.
Anna Margaret, daughter of Philip Maertz and Elizabeth, b. November 24, 1797, bapt. July 16, 1798. Spon: Parents.
Mary, daughter of James Davison and Louise, b. February 19, 1798, bapt. July 25, 1798. Spon: Parents.
Juliana, daughter of Michael Haas and Anna Maria, b. ----, bapt. July 25, 1798. Spon: Louise Davison and the Mother.
Anna Margaret, daughter of William Emis and Sarah, b. February 21, 1798, bapt. August 4, 1798. Spon: Valentine Kerper and Anna Margaret.
Marg. Catharine, daughter of Jacob Schlatter and Elizabeth, b. September 8, 1798, bapt. October 15, 1798. Spon: Margaret Losler.
Elizabeth, daughter of Philip Ferster and Elizabeth, b. September 7, 1798, bapt. ----, 1798. Spon: P. Thiel and Elizabeth.
David, son of Simon Friess and Margaret, b. August 30, 1798, bapt. ----, 1798. Spon: George Friess and wife, grandparents.
Anna Maria, daughter of John Hagy and Mary, b. ----, bapt. ----, 1798. Spon: ----.
Hannah, daughter of George Tress and Dorothea, b. September 12, 1796, bapt. ----, 1798. Spon: Parents.
George, son of George Tress and Dorothea, b. August 18, 1798, bapt. ----, 1798. Spon: Parents.
Joseph, son of George Friess and wife, b. May 8, 1793, bapt. October 16, 1798. Spon: G. Friess and wife, grandparents.
William, son of George Friess and wife, b. October 21, 1795, bapt. October 16, 1798. Spon: Parents.
Maria, daughter of George Friess and wife, b. February 23, 1798, bapt. October 16, 1798. Spon: Parents.
Joseph, son of Jacob Maurer and Esther, b. April 9, 1798, bapt. ----, 1798. Spon: Joseph Zeply and Mary Zeply.
Deborah, daughter of Casper Mayer and Mary, b. ----, bapt. October 14, 1798. Spon: Parents.
A child of William Stevenson and wife (Eleonore), b. ----, bapt.

October 14, 1798. Spon: Parents.
Mary, daughter of George Abel and Dorothea, b. September 10, 1793, bapt. October 15, 1798. Spon: Parents.
Anna Louise, daughter of Geo. Wm. Steinhauer and Catharine, b. July 21, 1798, bapt. October 21, 1798. Spon: Parents.
Joseph, son of Samuel Friess and wife, b. September 17, 1798, bapt. October 22, 1798. Spon: Parents.
Daniel, son of Daniel Hagy and Maria, b. November 19, 1797, bapt. October 22, 1798. Spon: Parents.
John, son of James Westword and Christine, b. October 11, 1798, bapt. October 22, 1798. Spon: Parents.
A child of ---- Kehr and wife, b. ----, bapt. October 22, 1798. Spon: Mr. Katz and wife.

1799
Hannah, daughter of Daniel Peltz and Susanna, b. August 18, 1798, bapt. October --, 1798. Spon: William Nicolaus and Hannah.
Deborah, daughter of ---- Rheiner and wife, b. September 1, 1798, bapt. December 6, 1798. Spon: Parents.
Maria, daughter of Jacob Tripler and Catharine, b. July 6, 1798, bapt. ----, 1798. Spon: Parents.
Hannah, daughter of George Bressler and Maria Catharine, b. December 11, 1798, bapt. January 20, 1799. Spon: Parents.
Anna Maria, daughter of John Kehrbach and Christine, b. November 10, 1798, bapt. February 10, 1799. Spon: The gather and Anna Maria Derr.
Margaret, daughter of John Nutz and Maria, b. February 2, 1799, bapt. February 10, 1799. Spon: Leonard Notz and Margaret, Grandparents.
Benjamin, son of William Hagy and Catharine, b. February 10, 1798, bapt. February 28, 1798. Spon: Parents.
George, son of Michael Lange and Margaret, b. January 19, 1799, bapt. March 2, 1799. Spon: Parents.
Hannah, daughter of ---- Staudt and wife, b. ----, bapt. March 26, 1799. Spon: Parents.
Philip, son of Justus Schuetz and Catharine, b. March 11, 1799, bapt. April 15, 1799. Spon: Parents.
Philip, son of Philip Schinkel and Catharine, b. May 27, 1799, bapt. September 11, 1799. Spon: ----.
Jesse, son of Abraham Selter and Margaret, b. February 8, 1799, bapt. April 23, 1799. Spon: Robert Thomas and Esther.
Sarah, daughter of Godfrey Bockius and Sally, b. December 9, 1798, bapt. April 26, 1799. Spon: Parents.
Susanna, daughter of Peter Weidner and Susanna, b. February 13, 1799, bapt. May 10, 1799. Spon: Parents.
A child of Stephen Singlewood and Anna, b. ----, bapt. May --, 1799. Spon: Parents.
Anna Barbara, daughter of Jacob Schaeffer and Margaret, b. April 1, 1799, bapt. May --, 1799. Spon: William Seyn and Anna Barbara.

Children of Joseph Miller and Susanna, bapt. May -- 1799:
Catharine, b. July 18, 1793.
Sarah, b. January 30, 1795.
Susanna, b. November 13, 1796.
Joseph, b. May 1, 1799. The parents were sponsors.

Jacob, son of Francis Bockius and Susanna, b. April 29, 1796, bapt. May --, 1799. Spon: Parents.
John, son of Christian Gutknecht and Elizabeth, b. August 6, 1798, bapt. May --, 1799. Spon: Parents.
Anna, daughter of Henry Kihly (Keely) and Elizabeth, b. November 20, 1795, bapt. May --, 1799. Spon: Parents.
Valentine, son of Henry Kihly (Keely) and Elizabeth, b. September 20, 1798, bapt. May --, 1799. Spon: Parents.
Jacob, son of Christopher Ossius and Elizabeth, b. March 5, 1799, bapt. May --, 1799. Spon: Parents.
Ornia (?), child of John Weber and Elizabeth, b. June 10, 1795, bapt. May --, 1799. Spon: William Seger and Anna Barbara.
Rosina, daughter of Peter Bockius and Rosina, b. June 2, 1795, bapt. May --, 1799. Spon: Parents.
Elizabeth, daughter of Jacob Miller and wife, b. September 1, 1798, bapt. May --, 1799. Spon: Parents.
Anthony, son of Anthony Gilbert and Elizabeth, b. August 26, 1794, bapt. May --, 1799. Spon: Parents.
William, son of John Rose and Mary, b. January 18, 1802, bapt. May 21, 1802. Spon: Parents.
Edmund, son of Etienne Dutilh and Catharine Magdalene, b. December 12, 1798, bapt. May 19, 1799. Spon: John Godfrey Wachsmuth, represented by Sarah Martineau.

Children of John Ross and Anna, bapt. May -- 1799. Spon: John Ross and wife Maria -
Sarah, b. February 7, 1788.
Phoebe (Feba), b. August 22, 1790.
Susanna, b. August 2, 1794.
Marianne, b. January 27, 1797.

Sally, daughter of John Schmidt and Elizabeth, b. September 10, 1796, bapt. May 20, 1799. Spon: Parents.

1800
William, son of Samuel Harkness and Catharine, b. November 15, 1799, bapt. August 10, 1800. Spon: ----.
Maria, daughter of John Lesley and Catharine, b. September 7, 1800, bapt. June 9, 1801. Spon: Parents.
Leonard, son of James Lovet and wife, b. November 10, 1799, bapt. October 19, ----. Spon: Leonard Notz and wife.
Anna, daughter of Henry Sorber and Catharine, b. January 1, 1800, bapt. July 8, 1801. Spon: Parents.
Martin, son of John Rose and Mary, b. January 20, 1800, bapt. March 2, ----. Spon: Parents.
The last five baptisms were entered by different hands.

Charlotte, daughter of James Hamilton and Elizabeth, b. April 15, 1800, bapt. September 21, 1800. Spon: Parents.
Anna, daughter of Joseph Rohrer and Catharine, b. December 18, 1799, bapt. September 21, 1800. Spon: Parents.
Elizabeth, daughter of Peter Schaarer and Catharine, b. September 16, 1799, bapt. ----, 1800. Spon: Parents.
Hester, daughter of John Rohrer and Margaret, b. July 6, 1788, bapt. ----, 1800. Spon: Parents.

Henry, son of John Davys and Margaret, b. August 10, 1799, bapt. October 4, 1801. Spon: Parents.
John, son of John Tripple and Catharine, b. September 2, 1800, bapt. October 4, 1801. Spon: Parents.
Mary, daughter of John Tripple and Catharine, b. July 6, 1798, bapt. October 4, 1801. Spon: Parents.
Mary, daughter of John Notz and Mary, b. July 11, 1801, bapt. October 4, 1801. Spon: John Lamb.
Marianne, daughter of Peter Kessler and Esther, b. April 7, 1801, bapt. October 4, 1801. Spon: Parents.

Baptisms by the Rev. John William Runkel, 1802-1806

Maria Catharine, daughter of Jacob Kerper and wife, b. October 1, 1799, bapt. September 22, 1800. Spon: Parents.
John, son of John Franck and Sarah, b. March 5, 1799, bapt. September 21, 1800. Spon: Parents.
These two baptisms are in the handwriting of Runkel but they belong probably to the ministry of Helffenstein.

Rachel, daughter of James Brown and Anna, b. April 25, 1800, bapt. April 4, 1802. Spon: Parents.
William, son of Christian Hollwe and Rosina, b. January 12, 1802, bapt. May 4, 1802. Spon: William Hollwe and Susanna.
Hannah and Maria, daughter of Valentine Wunder and Magdalene, b. December 15, 1801, bapt. May 9, 1802. Spon: Jacob Wunder and Hannah Maria.
Mary, daughter of John Howard and Rachel, b. April 13, 1802, bapt. May 23, 1802. Spon: John Meyweg.
Catharine, daughter of Samuel Person and Margaret, b. July 29, 1801, bapt. June 1, 1802. Spon: Parents.
Maria Anna, daughter of Philip Schinckel and Catharine, b. November 14, 1801, bapt. June 7, 1802. Spon: Elizabeth Stahr, widow.
John, son of Philip Fischer and Anna Maria, b. December 13, 1799, bapt. June 11, 1802. Spon: Parents.
Philip, son of Philip Fischer and Anna Maria, b. June 8, 1802, bapt. June 11, 1802. Spon: Parents.
William, son of Bernard Schuchard and Maria, b. May 20, 1802, bapt. June 30, 1802. Spon: Parents.
Maria, daughter of James Vannetta and Sarah, b. June 6, 1802, bapt. July 4, 1802. Spon: Parents.
Elizabeth, daughter of John Staut and Mary, b. March 16, 1797, bapt. July 13, 1802. Spon: Parents.
Hannah, daughter of John Staut and Mary, b. July 28, 1799, bapt. July 13, 1802. Spon: Parents.
Joseph, son of John Staut and Mary, b. September 4, 1801, bapt. July 13, 1802. Spon: Parents.
Alexander, son of Peter Hans and Elizabeth, b. April 25, 1802, bapt. August --, 1802. Spon: Parents.
George, son of Stephen Bo---- and Elizabeth, b. December 25, 1800, bapt. August 27, 1802. Spon: The Mother.
John, son of Joseph Miller and Susanna, b. April 2, 1802, bapt. September 6, 1802. Spon: Parents.
Michael, son of Michael Lewering and Catharine, b. June 14, 1799, bapt. September 7, 1802. Spon: Parents.
David, son of Michael Lewering and Catharine, b. June 14, 1788,

bapt. September 7, 1802. Spon: Parents.
Maria Dorothea, daughter of George Staub and Catharine, b. July 5, 1802, bapt. October 3, 1802. Spon: Parents.
Elizabeth, daughter of John Jacobi and Sophia, b. April 17, 1800, bapt. October 17, 1802. Spon: Parents.
Catharine, daughter of John Jacobi and Sophia, b. September 24, 1801, bapt. October 17, 1802. Spon: Parents.
Anna Elizabeth, daughter of William Hagy and Catharine, b. February 27, 1802, bapt. October 22, 1802. Spon: Parents.

Children of Philip Unruh and Barbara, bapt. November 2, 1802:
John, b. May 1, 1795.
Catharine, b. April 6, 1797.
Maria, b. August 7, 1799.
Jacob, b. December 5, 1801.
The parents were sponsors.

Robert, son of James Laird and Esther, b. July 8, 1802, bapt. November 4, 1804. Spon: Parents.
John, son of Jacob Miller and Anna, b. May 19, 1802, bapt. November 5, 1802. Spon: Parents.
William, son of Daniel Haegy and Magdalene, b. September 8, 1802, bapt. November 9, 1802. Spon: Parents and Widow Katz.
Joseph, son of William Carr and Maria, b. January 30, 1800, bapt. November 9, 1802. Spon: Parents.
Daniel, son of John Repein (Rehbein) and Anna, b. October 14, 1797, bapt. November 11, 1802. Spon: Parents.
Margaret, daughter of John Repein (Rehbein) and Anna, b. October 21, 1799, bapt. November 11, 1802. Spon: Parents.
Hannah, daughter of John Repein (Rehbein) and Anna, b. November 16, 1801, bapt. November 11, 1802. Spon: Parents.
Eli, son of Joseph Rohrer and Catharine, b. November 28, 1801, bapt. November 21, 1802. Spon: Parents.
Maria, daughter of John Reiner and Elizabeth, b. July 20, 1802, bapt. November 28, 1802. Spon: Parents.
Christine, daughter of Henry Ernst and Henrietta, b. November 15, 1802, bapt. December 7, 1802. Spon: Parents.

1803
Jacob, son of William Hoffman and Margaret, b. November 15, 1802, bapt. January 1, 1803. Spon: Parents.
Maria, daughter of Matthew Pearce and Mary, b. January 22, 1802, bapt. January 18, 1803. Spon: Parents.
George, son of Stephen Singlewood and Anna, b. June 17, 1802, bapt. January 27, 1803. Spon: Parents.
Esther, daughter of Joseph Hoh and Maria, b. December 27, 1802, bapt. February 13, 1803. Spon: Catharine Hoh, widow.
William, son of John Schmit and Elizabeth, b. April 17, 1801, bapt. March 17, 1803. Spon: Parents.
Elizabeth, daughter of Abraham Fahring and Elizabeth, b. June 13, 1802, bapt. April 10, 1803. Spon: Parents.
Francis William, son of Joseph Bockius and Margaret, b. December 10, 1802, bapt. April 10, 1803. Spon: Francis Bockius and Susanna.
Catharine, daughter of Daniel Kampman and Maria, b. February 28,

1801, bapt. April 26, 1803. Spon: Henry Baer and Marg., Elizabeth Kampman.

Elizabeth, daughter of Daniel Kampman and Maria, b. April 21, 1803, bapt. April 26, 1803. Spon: Henry Baer and Marg., Elizabeth Kampman.

Jacob, son of Jacob Windall and Elizabeth, b. June 12, 1792, bapt. May 17, 1803. Spon: The Mother.

Elizabeth, daughter of Jacob Windall and Elizabeth, b. September 22, 1794, bapt. May 17, 1803. Spon: The Mother.

Children of Abraham Paul and Barbara, bapt. May 29, 1803; parents were sponsors:
Daniel, b. December 20, 1792.
Abraham, b. December 6, 1794.
Sarah, b. March 19, 1799.
Jacob, b. April 15, 1801.
Anna Barbara, b. April 20, 1803.

Margaret, daughter of Jacob Guth and Elizabeth, b. January 8, 1795, bapt. May 29, 1803. Spon: Parents.

Margaret, daughter of Jacob Horter and Anna, b. January 26, 1802, bapt. May 29, 1803. Spon: John Bockius and Margaret.

John, son of Jacob Kiely and Elizabeth, b. April 9, 1803, bapt. May 29, 1803. Spon: Parents.

Rebecca, daughter of Samuel Diel and Margaret, b. May 25, 1803, bapt. June 9, 1803. Spon: Parents.

Samuel, son of Samuel Harkness and Catharine, b. November 24, 1802, bapt. June 10, 1803. Spon: Parents.

James, son of James McMullen and Martha, b. February 20, 1803, bapt. June 10, 1803. Spon: Parents.

George, son of John Ottison and Margaret, b. September 20, 1801, bapt. June 10, 1803. Spon: Parents.

Maria Catharine, daughter of Henry Davis and Maria Catharine, b. June 4, 1803, bapt. June 19, 1803. Spon: Parents.

George, son of Daniel Heller and Margaret, b. March 14, 1803, bapt. June 20, 1803. Spon: Parents.

Catharine, daughter of John Barral and Catharine, b. May 16, 1803, bapt. July 2, 1803. Spon: Parents.

Children of John Holbein and Eva, bapt. May 1, 1803; the parents were sponsors:
Susanna, b. October 14, 1797.
Catharine, b. May 30, 1799.
Samuel, b. February 7, 1801.
Elizabeth, b. November 19, 1802.

Sarah, daughter of George Jacob and Christine, b. October 1, 1802, bapt. July 20, 1803. Spon: Parents.

William, son of Jacob Staut and Tacy (Daisy), b. December 22, 1801.

Henry, son of George Staut and Mary, b. February 18, 1803, bapt. July 20, 1803. Spon: Parents.

William, son of John McBride and Catharine, b. July 1, 1802, bapt. July 24, 1803. Spon: Parents.

Josiah, son of Alexander Armor and Mary, b. September 9, 1802, bapt. August 5, 1803. Spon: Parents.

William, son of John Salter (deceased) and Mary, b. November 23, 1799, bapt. August 5, 1803. Spon: The Mother.
Susanna, daughter of Daniel Beltz and Susanna, b. August 3, 1803, bapt. September 4, 1803. Spon: Parents.
John, son of John Staut and Mary, b. June 3, 1803, bapt. September 14, 1803. Spon: Parents.
John, son of George Grees and Maria, b. August 21, 1803, bapt. September 18, 1803. Spon: John Wentzel and Elizabeth.
William, son of Peter Reisch and Sarah, b. ----, bapt. October 9, 1803. Spon: Jacob Fischer and Catharine.
Margaret, daughter of James Lovett and Christine, b. June 16, 1802, bapt. October 23, 1803. Spon: Leonard Notz and Margaret.
Susanna, daughter of Jacob Geissler and Hannah, b. October 28, ---, bapt. October 26, 1803. Spon: Parents.
Maria, daughter of Jacob Geissler and Hannah, b. June 2, ----, bapt. October 26, 1803. Spon: Parents.
Arthur Howel, son of John Nutz and Maria, b. October 20, 1803, bapt. November 6, 1803. Spon: Parents.
Emmanuel, son of Wm. Stevenson and Eleanor, b. July 30, 1800, bapt. November 15, 1803. Spon: Parents.
Edward, son of Wm. Stevenson and Eleanor, b. October 18, 1803, bapt. November 15, 1803. Spon: Parents.
Maria, daughter of Jacob Schlatter and Elizabeth, b. September 14, 1803, November 27, 1803. Spon: Parents.
Elizabeth, daughter of George Kerster and Margaret, b. September 20, 1798, bapt. November 28, 1803. Spon: Elizabeth Osman, wife of Capt. Osman, Veronica Keller.
Andrew, son of Andrew Hess and Susanna, b. November 16, 1803, bapt. November 30, 1803. Spon: Parents.
Anna Maria, daughter of Samuel Weber and Catharine, b. October 17, 1803, bapt. December 4, 1803. Spon: Parents.
Christine, daughter of Jacob Henn and Catharine, b. October 23, 1803, bapt. December 12, 1803. Spon: Christ. Voelcklein, single.
Rebecca, daughter of John Hazleton and Margaret, b. February 21, 1803, bapt. December 14, 1803. Spon: Parents.
Catharine, daughter of Christian Holbe and Rosina, b. January 29, 1802, bapt. January 15, 1804. Spon: Henry Werffel and Catharine.
Charles, son of Joseph Miller and Susanna, b. November 23, 1803, bapt. January 16, 1804. Spon: Parents.
Daniel, son of Jacob Kerper and Elizabeth, b. November 24, 1802, bapt. January 16, 1804. Spon: Parents.
Charles, son of George Kerper and Elizabeth, b. April 25, 1800, bapt. January 16, 1804. Spon: Parents.
Anna Maria, daughter of George Kerper and Elizabeth, b. October 20, 1802, bapt. January 16, 1804. Spon: Parents.
Joseph, son of Frederick Kerper and Christine, b. September 10, 1800, bapt. January 16, 1804. Spon: Parents.
Anna Maria, daughter of Frederick Kerper and Christine, b. August 3, 1802, bapt. January 16, 1804. Spon: Parents.
Henry, son of John Linck and Margaret, b. October 16, 1803, bapt. January 16, 1804. Spon: Parents.
Jacob, son of Martin Strauss and Regina, b. November 17, 1803, bapt. January 25, 1804. Spon: Jacob Strauss and Margaret.

Franklin, son of Daniel Tapham and Sarah, b. November 24, 1802, bapt. February 2, 1804. Spon: Godfrey Hoppe and A. Maria.
Sarah, daughter of John Tranck and Sarah, b. October 18, 1801, bapt. February 14, 1804. Spon: Parents.
George, son of John Baer and Maria, b. October 7, 1803, bapt. February 19, 1804. Spon: George Geisel and Magdalene.
James, son of Robert McGorge and Ann, b. March 6, 1804, bapt. March 18, 1804. Spon: Robert Thomson and Esther Thomson.
Maria, daughter of Abraham Seltzer and Margaret, b. December 21, 1803, bapt. March 18, 1804. Spon: Robert Thomson and Esther.
Anna, daughter of William Van Adam and Maria, wife of George Wunder, b. ----, 1756, bapt. March 30, 1804. Spon: Adult.
Margaret, daughter of Jacob Schneider and Anna Barbara, b. August 5, 1738, bapt. March 30, 1804. Spon: Adult.
Anna, daughter of Jacob Wunder and Susanna, b. August 16, 1803, bapt. April 2, 1804. Spon: George Wunder and Anna.
Anna, daughter of William Wunder and Catharine, b. February 23, 1804, bapt. April 2, 1804. Spon: George Wunder and Anna.
George Nice, son of William Notz and Susanna, b. May 20, 1804, bapt. June 24, 1804. Spon: George Notz.
Anthony, son of James Brown and Anna, b. June 3, 1804, bapt. July 8, 1804. Spon: Anthony Johns and Catharine.
Jacob, son of Michael Kehrbach and Catharine, b. March 8, 1804, bapt. July 21, 1804. Spon: Parents.
Jacob, son of Jacob Guth and Elizabeth, b. May 14, 1804, bapt. August 19, 1804. Spon: Parents.
Eloisa, daughter of George Miller and M. Margaret, b. January 1, 1800, bapt. August 24, 1804. Spon: Parents.
John Adams, son of George Miller and M. Margaret, b. May 30, 1803, bapt. August 24, 1804. Spon: Parents.
James, son of James Garner and Jane, b. October 4, 1803, bapt. August 26, 1804. Spon: Parents.
Robert, son of Robert Stewart and Mary, b. March 24, 1804, bapt. September 4, 1804. Spon: Parents.
Wm. Henry, son of Thomas Stewart and Abby, b. November 3, 1803, bapt. September 4, 1804. Spon: Parents.
Margaret, daughter of Henry Stewart and Margaret, b. August 27, 1804, bapt. September 4, 1804. Spon: The Father.
Henry, son of Harrison Spendlove and Martha, b. April 19, 1804, bapt. September 4, 1804. Spon: Parents.
Samuel, son of Joseph Bockius and Margaret, b. February 13, 1804, bapt. September 29, 1804. Spon: Parents.
Elizabeth, daughter of John Roos and Maria, b. July 19, 1804, bapt. October 14, 1804. Spon: Parents.

Children of Simon Fries and Margaret, bapt. October 31, 1804; the parents were sponsors.
Anna, b. February 5, 1800.
Charles, b. December 18, 1801.
Nicholas, b. November 9, 1803.

John, son of Peter Strieper and Ernestine, b. May 30, 1804, bapt. November 1, 1804. Spon: Parents.
Thomas, son of John Repein and Anna, b. November 4, 1803, bapt. November 1, 1804. Spon: The Father.

Susanna, daughter of Jacob Schaefer and Margaret, b. July 8, 1804, bapt. November 4, 1804. Spon: Rudolf Drach and Margaret.
Maria, daughter of Henry Rudy and Maria, b. November 1, 1804, bapt. November 5, 1804. Spon: Parents.
Elizabeth, daughter of John Hinckel and Elizabeth, b. October 20, 1803, bapt. November 5, 1804. Spon: Parents.
Margaret, daughter of Thomas Gentry and Margaret, b. May 17, 1804, bapt. November 11, 1804. Spon: George Caster.
Catharine Elizabeth, daughter of John Grafft Wunderlich and Catharine Elizabeth, b. October 31, 1804, bapt. November 13, 1804. Spon: The Father.
Wm. Henry, son of Joseph Sorber and Elizabeth, b. May 14, 1800, bapt. November 19, 1804. Spon: The Father.
Charles Kirk, son of Joseph Sorber and Elizabeth, b. April 3, 1802, bapt. November 19, 1804. Spon: The Father.
Jacob, son of R. Regenass and Magdalene, b. November 12, 1804, bapt. November 25, 1804. Spon: Elizabeth Rudy, single.
Jacob, son of George Kiel and Esther, b. December 10, 1800, bapt. December 2, 1804. Spon: Margaret Kiel, wife of Jacob.
John, son of George Kiel and Esther, b. June 6, 1803, bapt. December 2, 1804. Spon: John Kiel, single.

[From here on only baptisms for which births were 1800 or earlier. The following were baptized by Charles Helffenstein.]
Children of Christopher Wonner and Maria, bapt. October 19, 1806: Christianna, b. November 26, 1795; Judith, b. September 5, 1798; Catharine, b. December 3, 1800.

Children of George Peters and Elizabeth, bapt. March 29, 1807; the parents were sponsors: Abraham, b. October 20, 1794; Margaret, b. June 16, 1797; George, b. December 30, 1799; Samuel, b. August 22, 1789; Maria, b. September 22, 1787.

John Kile, son of Jesse (Kile) and Susanna, b. April 24, 1788, bapt. March 29, 1807. Spon: ----.

Children of Rudolp Frayley and Elizabeth, bapt. January 1, 1808; the parents were sponsors: Elizabeth, b. September 8, 1794; Catharine, b. November 22, 1796; Anna, b. September 8, 1798.

Children of Adam Bickard and Hannah, bapt. march 26, 1809; the parents were sponsors: Catharine, b. November 14, 1795; Betsie, b. December 8, 1797; Susan, b. November 8, 1800.

Children of Frederick Smith and wife, bapt. March 26, 1809: Catharine, b. December 26, 1792; Jacob, b. December 1, 1794; George, b. October 3, 17961 Valentine, b. January 1, 1799.

MARRIAGES

Marriages by the Rev. John Conrad Steiner, 1753 - 1756

Christian Geissler m. Sarah Reich on January 21, 1753.
Ulrich Freyhofer m. Magdalene Bechtel, both from Zurich, on January 25, 1753.
Ulrich Weidman, from Zurich, m. Anna Tschudi, from Basle, on January 28, 1753.
George Kenner, hatmaker, Lutheran, m. Magdalene Kress on February 25, 1753.
Conrad Maurer m. Susanna Buchmann, both from the Canton of Zurich, on February 26, 1753.
Rudolf Maurer m. Anna Mueller, both from Zurich, on April 15, 1753.
Jacob Sewer, from Bischweiler, m. Esther Welkin, widow of Jacob Welkin, residing in Upper Germantown, on April 16, 1753.
Andrew Koechlein, residing in Hilton Township m. Susanna Benner, daughter of the late John Benner of Hilton Township, on April 23, 1753.
George Allen, b. in Denmark, m. Susan Elizabeth Peierli on April 23, 1753.
John Meckendoerfer m. Maria Rosina Kern, widow of George Adam Kern, on April 23, 1753.
Jacob Mueller m. Christine Mueller, of New Providence, on May 4, 1753.
John Rudolf Maurer m. Anna Landis, from Canton of Zurich, on May 20, 1753.
Jean Bigonet, from Nimes, Languedoc, m. Cath. Elizabeth Osias, widow of Henry Osias, on May 27, 1753.
Jacob Baumann, cooper, m. Maria Barbara Herzbach on July 8, 1753.
Jacob Gerwer m. Mary Magdalene Rausch on July 18, 1753.
Jacob Weidmann m. Susanna Reyss on July 18, 1753.
Nicholas Heselbach m. Catharine Steiz on July 12, 1753.
Rudolf Huber m. Elizabeth Baer, from Zurich, on July 22, 1753.
Jacob Klein m. Elizabeth Keiser, Lutheran, on August 6, 1753.
Michael Weber m. Christina Gut, Lutheran, on September 12, 1753.
Rudolf Peter m. Susanna Hoffmann on September 16, 1753.
George Edelmann m. Anna Daegen on September 16, 1753.
Felix Dutweiler m. Elizabeth Schwenck on September 18, 1753.
Christopher Schmid m. Catharine Schlaegle on September 30, 1753.
George Seider m. Anna Margaret Reinhardt, Lutheran, on January 3, 1754.
Melchior Schwerer m. Rosina Freymath, Lutheran, on January 10, 1754.
John George Galfass m. Catharine Brumann on January 21, 1754.
Christian Schmid m. Catharine Elizabeth Becker on January 28, 1754.
Philip Hoffmann m. Anna Maria Kuenzler, Lutheran, on January 29, 1754.
Henry Naeff m. Joanna Steger on January 29, 1754.
Jacob Maurer m. Anna Wirth on February 5, 1754.
Rudolf Lang m. Sophia Seiffer on February 12, 1754.
John Erhardt m. Catharine Ostertey on February 24, 1754.
Casper Sorber m. Barbara Meyer on March 5, 1754.
Benjamin Essen m. Elizabeth Boltenstern on March 15, 1754.
John Schad m. Adelheid Mezenmacher on March 17, 1754.

John Jacob Scheich m. Anna Magdalene Grim, Lutheran, on March 28, 1754.
Sebastian Mueller m. Barbara Roesch on April 10, 1754.
Philip Himmelreich m. Hannah Dickesen on April 16, 1754.
Nicholas Heinrich m. Sophia Adams on May 5, 1754.
John Sorber and Anna Schwenck m. May 7, 1754.
Theobald Diehl m. Mary Magdalene Schirmer on May 7, 1754.
Martin Schlangenhuf and Margaret Lang on June 2, 1754.
John George Reichwein m. Susanna Weckerlin on June 30, 1754.
John Stump, Lutheran, m. Anna Maria Lintz on July 30, 1754.
Daniel Endt m. Catharine Zacharias on August 8, 1754.
Michael Schmidt m. Barbara Kuenzli on August 20, 1754.
John Binder m. Elizabeth Mueller on August 24, 1754.
William Coppin m. Anna Reynold on August 29, 1754.
John Knieriem m. Sophia Nold on September 8, 1754.
John Schroeder m. Ursula Keller on September 15, 1754.
Jacob Baer m. Barbara Krauer on September 30, 1754.
Godfrey Zeisinger m. Margaret Fehr on October 27, 1754.
John Jacob Sorber m. Anna Froeli on October 29, 1754.
Paulus Gross m. Maria Noth on December 24, 1754.
John Jetter m. Dorothea Schade on December 29, 1754.
Paulus Gerninger m. Elizabeth Schweizer on December 31, 1754.
Jacob Keyser m. Elizabeth Loescher on January 1, 1755.
John Adam Korel m. Elizabeth Jung on January 21, 1755.
Peter Ludwig Bockius m. Maria Mueller on February 6, 1755.
Michael Conrad m. Elizabeth Kuehn on February 11, 1755.
Philip Penter m. Susanna Baumanns on March 16, 1755.
Paulus Geisel m. Maria Margaret Mueller on March 16, 1755.
Elias Mistler m. Catharine Harlacher on April 6, 1755.
John George Binder m. Magdalene Weidmann on April 18, 1755.
Anthony Sulzer m. Maria Barbara Koehler on April 13, 1755.
Ludwig Baur m. Catharine Levering on May 15, 1755.
Christian Hoch m. Maria Catharine Horn on May 29, 1755.
John Philip Geil m. Mary Magdalene Burger on June 21, 1755.
John Casper Schlatter m. Barbara Merck on June 29, 1755.
John Michael Trappel m. Salome Moeller on July 4, 1755.
John Casper Scherer m. Barbara Zoebeli on July 31, 1755.
Henry Mitchet m. Catharine Trachsler on August 10, 1755.
John Jacob Geuscht m. Eva Catharine ---- on August 11, 1755.
Jeremiah Runkel m. Maria Catharine Moret on August 12, 1755.
Jacob Schmid m. Christine Mueller on August 12, 1755.
Nicholas Baserman m. Amelia Mond on September 14, 1755.
Michael Orner m. Maria Peyer on September 16, 1755.
Elias Gol m. Catharine Schneck on September 21, 1755.
William Lohmann m. Eva Geyer on September 26, 1755.
John Peter Heiss m. Catharine Stillwagen on September 30, 1755.
David Journal m. Anna Maria Freylive on October 16, 1755.
Peter Meyer m. Margaret Karst on October 12, 1755.
John Peter Schmid m. Maria Elizabeth Binder on October 19, 1755.
Isaac Burgum m. Maria Elizabeth Pauser on November 2, 1755.
Adam Eckart m. Anna Catharine Maderi on November 18, 1755.
John Adam Lentz m. Anna Barbara Werner on November 24, 1755.
John Jacob Mitschet m. Catharine Margaret Trachsler on November 25, 1755.
Samuel Detterling m. Margaret Brey on November 27, 1755.

John Michael Seifried m. Catharine Peters on November 29, 1755.
Andrew Heyl m. Elizabeth Hercher on November 30, 1755.
John Wendel Pritius m. Christine Steiner on December 14, 1755.
John Hegins m. Anna Elizabeth Kerner on December 21, 1755.
Richard De m. Maria Barbara Kapp on December 8, 1755.
James Engle m. Barbara Weidner on December 27, 1755.
Peter Ochs m. Elizabeth Neiss on January 15, 1756.
John Valentine Kern m. Anna Margaret Schmid on January 18, 1756.
John Peter Tranck m. Mary Magdalene Elsheimer on January --, 1756.
Martin Binder m. Elizabeth Binder on February 3, 1756.
Jacob Naef m. Anna Buser on February 3, 1756.
Michael Bloch m. Mary Magdalene Leebrock on February 3, 1756.
John George Braunsberg m. Anna Falkenstein on February 3, 1756.
Henry Godfrey Dill m. Christine Litsch on February 27, 1756.
William Redinhaus m. Susanna Maurer on March 7, 1756.
John Jacob Meracher m. Anna Graf on March 15, 1756.
Edward Tilly m. Anna Elizabeth Knaus on April 3, 1756.
Philip Roerig m. Elizabeth Kemer on April 3, 1756.
John Jacob Renner m. Anna Margaret Bast on April 11, 1756.
Rudolf Widmer m. Elizabeth Baur on April 19, 1756.
John Conrad Brozmann m. Anna Kunigunda Eschbach on April 22, 1756.
Henry Stump m. Anna Maria Klaus on April 22, 1756.
Henry Bauser m. Catharine Zoebeli on April 26, 1756.
John Sorber m. Elizabeth Sorber on May 11, 1756.
John Jacob Ache m. Anna Maria Till on June 2, 1756.
Jacob Han m. Susanna Regina Gauss on June 6, 1756.

Marriages by the Rev. John Geo. Alsentz, 1758 - 1767

George Michael Gamber, widower, m. Elizabeth Mueller, single, on March 19, 1758.
Jacob Schreiner m. Dorothy Meng on March 30, 1758.
Peter Straub m. Catharine Armin on April 4, 1758.
John Heisch m. Catharine Koomin on May 15, 1758.
Conrad Kemp m. Veronica Kohl on June 4, 1758.
Valentine Hiss m. Maria Christine Boerner on July 4, 1758.
Benjamin Howel m. Maria Elizabeth Beest on August 8, 1758.
George Braun m. Joanna Elizabeth Tranck on September 10, 1758.
Michael Simon m. Catharine Weibel, both widowed, on October 24, 1758.
Isaac Budeman m. Maria Hueler on November 3, 1758.
Engelbert Dinges m. Anna Maria Swiney on December 30, 1758.
Jacob Schaub m. Elizabeth Scheppy, both single, on January 1, 1759.
George Philip Seybold m. Anna Maria Becker on February 6, 1759.
Peter Staud m. Barbara Nesterlin on February 11, 1759.
Jacob Ziĕt m. Margaret Geisel on February 13, 1759.
Peter Bigler m. Dorothea Heiberger, in Philadelphia, on February 18, 1759.
Abraham Hegely m. Anna Maria Runkel, both single, on February 18, 1759.
Benjamin Hellings m. Sidonia Shirradt on February 25, 1759.
Simon Peter Reiss m. Anna Barbara Delker on February 27, 1759.
Francis Schaefer m. Elizabeth Kehler, in Philadelphia, on March 18, 1759.
Conrad Duepo m. Esther Ammon, in Philadelphia, on March 25, 1759.
Jacob Whartnaby m. Barbara Power, in Abenton (Abingdon), on April

9, 1759.

John Henry Moritz m. Maria Jeanetta Schmid, in Philadelphia, on April 10, 1759.

John Matthias Mueller m. Anna Margaret Ries on April 16, 1759.

Herman Gerlach m. Catharine Morchel on April 16, 1759.

John Granadier m. Elizabeth Ries, in Frankford, on April 16, 1759.

George Adams m. Elizabeth Schneider on April 16, 1759.

Joseph Knaus m. Anna Margaret Zell, in Whitemarsh, on April 18, 1759.

George Peter Bock m. Mary Magdalene Schuetz, in Worcester, on April 19, 1759.

Daniel Bernthaler m. Anna Gertrude Klimken, in Whitemarsh, on May 15, 1759.

Abraham Henrich m. Elizabeth Weber, both widowed, on May 15, 1759.

John Peil m. Maria Schmid, in Merion, on June 12, 1759.

Jacob Scheutz m. Veronica Eterd, in Whitemarsh, on July 31, 1759.

David Hungerbiler m. Anna Mayer, Philadelphia and Scheltenheim, on May 29, 1759.

John Stuber m. Elizabeth Von der Linden, in Whitemarsh, on September 18, 1759.

John Peter Banno m. Anna Elizabeth Ries, in Germantown, on October 21, 1759.

Nicholas Rebein m. Sophia Hettebach, in Roxbury, on October 29, 1759.

Christopher Meng m. Catharine Gensel, in Germantown, both widowed, on September 13, 1759.

John August Straube m. Catharine Elizabeth Leitzebach, in Whitemarsh, on October 7, 1759.

Bartholomew Lamm m. Maria Catharine Rinn, both widowed, on December 2, 1759.

Casper Fahnstecke m. Catharine Cleim, in Germantown, on December 3, 1759.

Nicholas Schreiner m. Maria Gamper, in Philadelphia, on January 6, 1760.

John George Krieger m. Maria Haven, both in Whitpain, on February 17, 1760.

Daniel Joost m. Elizabeth Sperr, in Worcester, on February 21, 1760.

Peter Geraw m. Elizabeth Otto, both widowed, in Germantown, on March 30, 1760.

Christian Jauch m. Mary Magdalene Stortz, in Germantown, on April 13, 1760.

John Licht m. Agnes Rau, in Germantown, on April 27, 1760.

John Zumbro m. Maria Elizabeth Wisser, in Worcester, on May 6, 1760.

Peter Wolff m. Juliana Catharine Schmell, in Worcester, on May 15, 1760.

Peter Weissman m. Elizabeth Margaret Hemm, in Germantown, June 24, 1760.

George Philip Heitschu m. Catharine Maria Repoll on June 29, 1760.

Peter Rush m. Elizabeth Miller, in Creasham Township, on July 17, 1760.

Andrew Kern m. Catharine Hoffman, in Marion, on August 5, 1760.

David Dauderman m. Christine Rick, both widowed, in Germantown, on September 25, 1760.

Rudolf Zuebly m. Elizabeth Kern, in Blokly and Merion Township, on September 30, 1760.
John Johnston m. Anna Davis, in the Northern Liberties, on October 5, 1760.
Lawrence Walter m. Anna Margaret Hard, in Toyamensing Township, on October 20, 1760.
John George Edelman m. Anna Miller, in Springfield Township, on October 30, 1760.
Jacob Ringer m. Anna Maria Veronica Staehelin, in Chestnut Hill, on November 6, 1760.
John Henry Fenner m. Maria Cath. Schmell, in Worcester, on November 17, 1760.
John Martin Mayer m. Anna Magdalene Rucker, in Whitemarsh, on November 23, 1760.
Henry Schad m. Christine Stoes, in Northern Liberties, on December 23, 1760.
John Ries m. Catharine Hoehl, in Frankford, on January 5, 1761.
Bernard Matthaeus m. Anna Elizabeth Gebhard, in Germantown, on January 11, 1761.
Frederick Schneider m. Barbara Wanner, in Germantown, on January 27, 1761.
Jacob Mayer m. Barbara Kuebler, Gresham and Cheltenheim Township, on February 17, 1761.
Frederick Klaer m. Regina Wolfskehl, in Worcester Township, on March 1, 1761.
Matthew Stimme m. Christine Hill, in Philadelphia, on March 17, 1761.
Jacob Maurer m. Christine Kampmann, Northern Liberties, on March 24, 1761.
John Frederick Bast, m. Elizabeth Adams, Germantown, on March 24, 1761.
Valentine Scherer m. Anna Maria Knsel, in Whitpain, on April 6, 1761.
Philip Achenbach m. Margaret Kamm, Germantown, on April 7, 1761.
Jacob Hauser m. Anna Margaret Schott, Gresham Township, on May 26, 1761.
Herman Ache m. Maria Paulina Puff, Upper Dublin, on May 28, 1761.
Daniel Kampman m. Elizabeth Maurer, Northern Liberties, on June 2, 1761.
Balthasar Eckard m. Maria Strohauer, Germantown, on June 2, 1761.
John George Krueger m. Catharine Dorst, both widowed, Germantown, on June 7, 1761.
Jacob Kopp m. Anna Margaret Engert, Upper Dublin, on June 30, 1761.
John William Kampman m. Anna Margaret Pilgrim, Northern Liberties, on August 9, 1761.
Henry Walton m. Rebecca Van Sant, Smithfield Township, on August 9, 1761.
John George Croneiss m. ---- on October 12, 1762.
John Weber m. Veronica Miller, Worcester Township, on December 19, 1762.
John Peter Weckerle m. Catharine Margaret Kerbach, Bristol Township, March 17, 1763.
John George Strehle m. Maria Suter, widow, in Germantown, on March 29, 1763.
Valentine Stellwagen m. Elizabeth Steinmetz, Philadelphia, on May

3, 1763.
Conrad Becker m. Anna Maria Bumm, on the Point, on June 7, 1763.
John Miller m. Margaret Campbell, Germantown, on May 12, 1763.
Jacob Kopp m. Veronica Hang, both widowed, in Upper Dublin, on April 9, 1763.
Lewis Schneider m. Caty Dommet, Springfield Township, on July --, 1763.
Matthew Kayser m. Hester Belitz, both widowed, in Germantown, on July 13, 1763.
Philip Will m. Charlotta Gensel, Germantown, August 18, 1763.
William Dubre m. Mary Marten, Northern Liberties, August 25, 1763.
Frederick Tussy m. Susanna Dirrickson, New Castle, on September 13, 1763.
Jacob Frederick Faht m. Barbara Schmid, Worcester Township, on September 29, 1763.
John Grimm m. Catharine Sehn, Cheltenham Township, on November 15, 1763.
James Chalmers m. Margaret Jekyll, Philadelphia, on December 19, 1763.
George Gardner m. Joanna Printel, Germantown, on February 14, 1764.
George Sterner m. Barbara Geyger, both widowed, Germantown, on February 16, 1764.
George Hargisheimer m. Rosina Rumisperger, Philadelphia, on February 21, 1764.
Christian Saenger m. Hannah Peters, Witpen Township, on February 23, 1764.
Samuel Runckel m. Catharine Edert, Witpen Township, on February 23, 1764.
Henry Schuetz m. Catharine Rubenkamp, Springfield Township, on March 29, 1764.
Joseph Ellis m. Sarah Hugg, West New Jersey, on April 9, 1764.
William Naesch m. Rachel Hendriks on April 10, 1764.
Frederick Gerster m. Elizabeth Rohre, Oxford Township, on April 10, 1764.
John Weydmann m. Eva Catharine Streby, Gresham Township, on May 1, 1764.
George Sebastian Unruh m. Catharine Simon, Gresham Township, on June 17, 1764.
Daniel Wickert m. Maria Morris, Skippack Township, on August 14, 1764.
Henry Kuntz m. Kunigunda Hechtold, Springfield Township, on August 14, 1764.
Henry Peter Grimm m. Dorothea Sophia Hein, Philadelphia, on August 20, 1764.
Humphrey Chillcott m. Jane Davidson, Abington Township, on September 20, 1764.
William McKennery m. Eleanor Johnson, Philadelphia, on August 28, 1764.
Bernard Kuter m. Anna Maria Hoffmann, Springfield Township, on November 7, 1764.
John Michael Alt m. Maria Elizabeth Nisley, Germantown, on November 7, 1764.
Henry Engert m. Rachel Atkins, Upper Dublin on November 7, 1764.
John Jacob Kerbach m. Catharine Bikes, Germantown, on November 7, 1764.

David Paul m. Catharine Gysbert, Limerick Township, on October 14, 1764.
John George Alsentz, pastor of Germantown, m. Barbara Wentz, in Worcester Township by the Rev. Mr. Weyberg, on December 11, 1764.
Henry Krebs, widower, m. Veronica Zimmermann, Whitpain, on January 1, 1765.
John Nicholas Billman m. Elizabeth Bauer, Germantown, on January 15, 1765.
Henry Simon m. Elizabeth Schaefer, Germantown, on February 24, 1765.
John Surber m. Magdalene Zorn, both of Germantown, on February 26, 1765.
William Till m. Anna Mayer, both of Germantown, on March 21, 1765.
Christopher Groskoop m. Margaret Kayser, Gresham Township, on April 30, 1765.
John Thompson m. Mary Haly, both of Germantown, on May 3, 1765.
John Peter Leske m. Margaret Linenschiet on May 30, 1765.
John Umstätt m. Sybilla Boors, Skippack, on July 2, 1765.
George Gerster m. Margaret Shuebely, Germantown, on July 9, 1765.
Jacob Renner m. Elizabeth Kohler, Worcester Township, on July 18, 1765.
Henry Bamberger m. ---- on September --, 1765.
John Ary Koch m. ---- on October --, 1765.
William Collody m. Hannah Pastorius, Germantown, on October 17, 1765.
Melchior Meng m. Elizabeth Ax, Germantown, both widowed, on November 23, 1765.
Conrad Lieser m. Christine Steitel, Germantown, on November 26, 1765.
Peter Schuch m. Veronica Angst, Worcester, on November 26, 1765.
Peter Steidler m. Maria Eva Ulmer, Upper Merian, on December 5, 1765.
Owen Degharty m. Catharine Waltzner, Springfield, on January 14, 1766.
Michael Furman m. Elizabeth Davis, Blockly Township, on February 6, 1766.
James Stringer m. Mary Wright, Bristol, on February 9, 1766.
Jacob Saenger m. Margaret Bock, Worcester, on February 11, 1766.
John Casper Hoffmann m. Anna Maria Kraft, both widowed, Philadelphia, on February 23, 1766.
Matthias Nion m. Mary Swim, Springfield, on February 25, 1766.
Adam Renner m. Regina Schener, Worcester, on April 1, 1766.
Jacob Kark m. Anna Evans, Lower Merion Township, on April 3, 1766.
Casper Zilling m. Catharine Lefeber, Worcester, on April 8, 1766.
John William Kreiter m. Magdalene Reinhard, Worcester, on April 29, 1766.
Abraham Hendrick m. Magdalene Godschalk, Towamensing, on May 20, 1766.
George Walther m. Margaret Groskopp, Germantown, on May 20, 1766.
Leonard Redling m. Elizabeth Gibbs, Whitemarsh, on August 5, 1766.
John Adam Greim m. Maria Elizabeth Schneider, Springfield, on August 7, 1766.
Conrad Lindner m. Barbara Davis, Philadelphia, on ----, 1766.
Richard Martin m. Martha Leech, Cheltenham, on June 12, 1766.

Abraham Tuley m. Hannah Slicer on October 10, 1766.
Jacob Schneider m. Elizabeth Sickle, Philadelphia, on November 4, 1766.
Robert Allison m. Rachel Gunning, Philadelphia, on December 2, 1766.
John Murray m. Hannah Lindley on December 18, 1766.
Theobald Ent, Jr. m. Maria Barbara Haas, Germantown, on December 18, 1766.
John George Schneider m. Maria Verena Bilger, widow, Bristol, on January 29, 1767.
John Feigner m. Maria Sarah Faerner, widow, Germantown, on February 26, 1767.
John Henry Ederisch m. Elizabeth Eicher, Whitpain, on March 17, 1767.
Valentine Horder m. Mary Magdalene Reuss, Germantown, on April 2, 1767.
William Pannebecker m. Anna Maria Haas, Skippack, on April 20, 1767.
Carl Haaf m. Elizabeth Schambach, Limerick Township, on April 20, 1767.
Philip Miller m. Catharine Kohler, Worcester, on April 21, 1767.
Philip Saenger m. Philippina Werkhaeuser, Worcester, on April 21, 1767.
John Beth m. Barbara Simon, Germantown, May 20, 1767.
John Kerbach m. Dorothea Gardner, Germantown, both widowed, on May 28, 1767.
John Roth m. Anna Margaret Zeller on June 15, 1767.
John Dedier m. Susanna Ernst, widowed, Germantown, on June 16, 1767.
Isaac Rausch m. Anna Deschler, both single, on July 14, 1767.
This marriage was entered by John C. Faber.

Marriages by the Rev. Christian F. Foehring, 1769 - 1772

John Philip Kresman m. Maria Elizabeth Gerster, Oxford Township, on May 9, 1769.
George Wiester m. Juliana Leitner, Philadelphia, on May 7, 1769.
John Lamb m. Maria Cline, Germantown, on May 27, 1769.
David Mack m. Anna Wackerley, Springfield Township, on August 15, 1769.
John Frely m. Christine McCall, Germantown, on December 18, 1769.
Henry Hoffman m. Maria Solomey, Germantown, second marriage, on January 1, 1770.
Felix Liebestein, widower, m. Apollonia Leidi, Gresham, on April 8, 1770.
Matthias Martin m. Barbara Traxel, Whitpain, on April 24, 1770.
Christopher Henrici m. Elizabeth Gutknecht, Germantown, on April 24, 1770.
Jacob Wentz m. Barbara Alsentz, widow, on June 22, 1770.
John Traxel m. Elizabeth Martin, both single, on August 28, 1770.
John Sanger m. Margaret Bauer on September 25, 1770.
John Strieper m. Deborah Levering on January 24, 1771.
David Mueller m. Christine Blecker, Germantown, March 12, 1771.
Jacob Evans m. Hannah Morris, Whitpain, on March 16, 1771.
Henry Funck m. Anna Margaret Karch on March 26, 1771.
Thomas Cox m. Rachel White on March 28, 1771.

John George Edrige m. Martha Egbord on April 2, 1771.
John Fleck m. Mary Fries on April 9, 1771.
Frederick Kally m. Hester Lagman on April 9, 1771.
Theodore Groscop m. Elizabeth Rack on May 26, 1771.
Jacob Cowelens m. Elizabeth Shoeman on June 30, 1771.
Gerhard Hud m. Maria Wentz on July 3, 1771.
John Neweling m. Catharine Steinmetz on September 10, 1771.
John Dull m. Elizabeth McMeal on September 26, 1771.
Jacob Smith m. Margaret Draxel on October 15, 1771.
Joseph Fry m. Elizabeth Hoffman on October 17, 1771.
Samuel Willis m. Elizabeth Lucken, both of Germantown, on October 29, 1771.
Sebastian Fawst m. Anna Elizabeth Ritter on November 19, 1771.
John Hosford m. Hannah Kelly on November 24, 1771.
Hugh Baker m. Mary Cousens on December 15, 1771.
Philip Ewalt m. Hannah Ott, Rocksberry Township, on January 1, 1772.
Jonah Yokum m. Hannah Coler, Northern Liberties, Philadelphia, on February 4, 1772.
Jacob Rode m. Susanna Weidtman, widow, on February 23, 1772.
John Conrad m. Phobe Lies, both single, on February 29, 1772.
Jacob Wynkoop m. Hannah Cleaver, Philadelphia Co., on March 13, 1772.
Henry Sebold m. Ann Bilby, Germantown, on April 12, 1772.
Benjamin Teison m. Dorothea Morgan, Philadelphia, on April 14, 1772.

Marriages by J. C. Albert Helffenstein, 1772 - 1775

Joseph Boys m. Barbara Heffelinger, Skippack, on May 18, 1772.
John Adams m. Catharine Hummers, at Leisens, on August 20, 1772.
John Adams, Germantown, m. Catharine Hammer on August 21, 1772.
Stephan Feil m. Elizabeth Daudermann, both of Germantown, on September 27, 1772.
John Redebach m. Magdalene Bedillion on October 6, 1772.
John Michael Mischert m. Catharine Reiss, Germantown, on October 20, 1772.
Henry Beck, of Germantown, m. Catharine Ernst on March 9, 1773.
Michael Simon, of Gresham, m. Anna Rubenkamm on March 14, 1773.
Adam Becker, of Frankford, m. Elizabeth Naeff on March 16, 1773.
Philip Conrad m. Catharine Froelich on March 26, 1773.
Jacob Haas m. Anna Maria Karst, Northern Liberties, on April 6, 1773.
Jacob Bossert m. Mary Magdalene Frey, Northern Liberties, on January 3, 1775.
John Jegel m. Maria Schlauch, Philadelphia, on February 26, 1775.
Godfrey Miller, of Whitemarsh, m. Maria Faringer, of Upper Dublin, on May 4, 1775.
Thomas Wallis, of Frederickstown, MD, m. Maria Gottwald, of Germantown, on May 7, 1775.

Marriages by Rev. Samuel Dubbendorff, 1777 - 1779

George Kremer m. Catharine Schaur on August 7, 1777.
William Klein m. Cath. Gleim on August 7, 1777.
Paul Bischer m. Margaret Oberlaender on August 7, 1777.
Adam Enger m. Anna Cath. Schwerer on August 7, 1777.

Anthony Muth m. Widow Moor on January 4, 1778.
John Kocher m. Martha Willes on February 5, 1778.
John Gilmer m. Sarah Tempelton on February 5, 1778.
William Bartholomei m. Sibylla Evett on February 17, 1778.
John George Conrad Schwertmiller m. Maria Behler on February 19, 1778.
John Tibben m. Cath. Levering on April 20, 1778.
David Merethel m. Sophia Lehman on May 7, 1778.
David Thomson m. Mary Adams on July 19, 1778.
John George Wahrfield m. Maria Sybilla Krombert on July 28, 1778.
John Schuster m. Elizabeth Schmidt on August 27, 1778.
John Frederick Grap m. Fanny Meyer on September 29, 1778.
John George Steffen m. Cath. Wissler on November 19, 1778.
George Bressler m. Catharine Knorr on November 21, 1778.
William Pitt m. Elizabeth Schlossman on January 17, 1779.
John Benner m. Maria Schuster on April 20, 1779.
Henry Schnabel m. Veronica Matthaeus on September 19, 1779.
George Kocher m. Marg. Mayer on November 7, 1779.
Valentine Baeck m. Catharine Weidner on November 16, 1779.
Richard Bichen m. Sarah Martin on November 16, 1779.

Marriages by J. C. Albert Helffenstein, 1785 - 1790. Entered by Mr. Herman.
George Knorr m. Elizabeth Schuetz on December 23, 1785.
Henry Schuetz m. Elizabeth Hacker on May 12, 1786.
Justus Schutz m. Catharine Opman on March 10, 1789.
John Schlatter m. Catharine Schuetz on March 4, 1790.
Jacob Heller m. Miss Margaret Schuetz on November 26, 1795, by Mr. Herman, pastor loci.

Marriages by L. Frederick Herman, V.D.M.
Christian Lehman m. Sybilla Doll on December 18, 1790.
David Henrich m. Maria Schettinger on February 1, 1791.
Jacob Barrall m. Dorothea Geissler on February 3, 1791.
Henry Schermer m. Maria Kerber on March 1, 1791.
Ulrich Schutz m. Susanna Hilligard on March 1, 1791.
Jacob Geissler m. Hannah Gebler on April 12, 1791.
John Ashmead m. Hany Reiter, Germantown, on April 17, 1791.
Christopher Wunter m. Maria Antes on April 19, 1791.
Alexander Cassey m. Nancy Lotz on April 20, 1791.
John Corwell m. Barbara Lin on May 12, 1791.
John Beyls m. Sally Taylor on June 7, 1791.
John Rose m. Maria Weaver, in Philadelphia, on March 30, 1798 by the Rev. Mr. Carline.

[There are no marriages recorded from March 30, 1798 through 1800.]

BURIAL RECORDS

Burials by the Rev. John George Alsentz, 1758 - 1764

Matthew Schwartz, 65 years old, buried March 17[12?], 1758.
John George Ries, 1 year, 4 months old, buried March 26, 1758.
Elizabeth Schuetz, 9 years, 2 months, 3 weeks old, daughter of Henry, buried June 26, 1758.

John Peter Schuster, 12 years old, drowned, buried July 17, 1758.
Anna Maria Henrich, wife of Abraham Henrich, 41 years, 9 months old, buried August 11, 1758.
Elizabeth Barbara Simon, wife of Michael Simon, 48 years old, buried August 28, 1758.
Christopher Funck, 5 years, 8 months, 8 days old, buried September 9, 1758.
Peter Does, 52 years old, buried September 18, 1758.
---- Schneider, 12 years old, buried September 23, 1758.
Anna Eva Gardner, 56 years old, buried September 24, 1758.
---- Gardner, son of Anna Eva Gardner, 20 years old, buried September 24, 1758.
Anna Reebein, 15 years, 8 months old, buried September 25, 1758.
Sebastian Reebein, 9 years, 6 days old, buried September 25, 1758.
Susanna Graff, 23 years old, buried September 26, 1758.
Seyfert Gaertz, in Kensington, 29 years old, buried September 28, 1758.
Jacob Reebein, 6 years old, buried October 2, 1758.
Barbara Baer, wife of Jacob Baer, 23 years old, buried October 3, 1758.
Peter Theophilus Gilbert, 9 years, 8 months, 16 days, buried October 5, 1758.
Maria Margaret Reebein, wife of Nich. Reebein, 47 years old, buried October 11, 1758.
Henry Summer, 55 years old, killed by a horse, buried October 19, 1758.
Jacob Schwenck, 64 years, less 2 weeks old, buried January 4, 1759.
John Adam Seybold, 1 year, 6 months, 18 days old, buried March 22, 1759.
John Rebold, 1 year, 7 days old, buried March 27, 1759.
Joanna Elizabeth Franck, 2 years, 1 month old, buried April 9, 1759.
John George Reiff, 65 years old, buried April 21, 1759.
Maria Budeman buried May 13, 1759.
Eva Butta, wife of George Butta, 70 years old, buried ----, 1759.
John Adam Oberlaender, 1 year, 1 day old, buried June 3, 1759.
Henry Straub, 26 years old, buried August 28, 1759.
Joseph Staely, 49 years old, buried September 4, 1759.
David Engert, 20 weeks old, buried September 5, 1759.
Barbara Dommet, wife of Christian Dommet, 16 years, 10 months old, buried September 5, 1759.
Mary Magd. Frank, wife of Peter Frank, 39 years old, buried September 9, 1759.
Maria Barbara Heins, 5 months old, buried September 10, 1759.
Peter Güttinger, 1 year, 9 months, 10 days old, buried September 13, 1759.
Jacob Doenig, 2 years, 4 months old, buried September 17, 1759.
Jonathan Klinck, 1 year, 1 month old, buried November 10, 1759.
Henry Merke, 29 years old, married, buried November 18, 1759.

1760
Elizabeth Kuebeler, 1 year, 9 days old, buried January 15, 1760.
John Godfrey Thiel, 4 years, 7 weeks 1 day old, buried January 22, 1760.
Anna Maria Resch, 62 years, 9 months old, buried March 28, 1760.

John Wildfang, 2 years, 11 months old, buried March 30, 1760.
Anna Maria Bickes, 1 year, 2 months old, buried April 2, 1760.
Maria Krueger, 50 years old, in Whitpain, buried April 11, 1760.
Anna Barbara Schneider, 50 years, 4 months old, buried May 11, 1760.
Susanna Engle, about 2 years old, buried May 30, 1760.
John Kegy, 4 years, 10 months old, buried June 26, 1760.
---- Rapp, 3 years, 3 months old, buried July 7, 1760.
---- Jentzer, wife of Christian Jentzer, -- years old, buried July --, 1760.
---- Fries, 1 year old girl, buried June 31, 1760.
John George Otto, 4 years old, buried August 1, 1760.
Jacob Reboul, 48 years, 20 days old, buried August 28, 1760.
Tobias Adam Mayer, 2 years, 6 months old, buried August 31, 1760.
John Hartman Reboul, 3 months old, buried October 12, 1760.
Arnold Rittershahn, 71 years and some months old, in Whitpain, buried January 16, 1761.
Elizabeth Naglee, wife of Jacob Naglee, 36 years old, buried January 18, 1761.
Henry Ernst, 50 years and some months old, buried January 19, 1761.
Anna Martha Hangin, 25 years, 4 months old, in Whitpain, buried January 21, 1761.
An Englishman, 89 years old, in Germantown, buried February 1, 1761.
---- (Mrs.) Mayer, wife of Henry Mayer, 32 years old, buried March 13, 1761.
Margaret Ehmann, wife of ---- Ehmann, 51 years old, buried April 3, 1761.
Elizabeth Frank, daughter of Peter Frank, 9 months old, buried August 8, 1761.
John Philip Wunderlich, 2 years, 8 months old, buried August 8, 1761.
Jacob Weidman, about 60 years old, buried September 7, 1762.
Benjamin Engle, 44 years old, buried December 3, 1762.
David Suter, 52 years old, buried February 3, 1763.
Christian Peter, 27 years old, buried March --, 1763.
Elizabeth Meklen, 2 years old, buried April 22, 1763.
John Poet, 41 years old, buried April 23, 1763.
Elizabeth Reindaler, 5 years old, buried April 30, 1763.
Henry Bitting, 5 years, 4 months old, buried May 2, 1763.
Susanna Spira, 1 year, 1 month old, buried May 2, 1763.
Sarah Neiss, 21 years old, buried May 18, 1763.
Catharine Rupp, 5 years, 6 months old, buried June 2, 1763.
Jacob Reinthaler, 2 years, 6 weeks old, buried May 20, 1763.
John Andrae, 1 year, 3 weeks old, buried June 18, 1763.
Judith Schumacher, 24 years old, buried June 18, 1763.
William Schneider, 67 years old, buried August --, 1763.
Henry, William and Joseph Dusten, 3 children of one father, buried January 4, 1764.
Maria Ent, 2 years, 5 months old, buried January 15, 1764.
George Bockius, 7 years old, buried February 28, 1764.
John ----, 8 years old, buried February 17, 1764.
Maria Meng, 1 year, 5 months old, buried February 14, 1764.
Anna Maria Bickes, 4 years old, buried February 16, 1764.
John Findele, 9 years 6 weeks old, buried February 17, 1764.

"Catalog of Deceased continued by Albert Helffenstein, P.t. Pastor."

Catharine Staup, 6 months old, buried June 6, 1772.

Christian Koerback, 64 years old, buried July 15, 1772.

Conrad Schweitzer, 63 years old, buried July 15, 1772.

Anna Engel, 44 years, 6 months, 2 days old, buried August 8, 1772.

John Conrad Weil, Frankfurt, 49 years old, buried August 5, 1772.

Peter ----, Frankfurt, 58 years old, buried September 5, 1772.

Valentine Gilbert, Philadelphia, Lutheran, 14 years, 2 months old, buried September 7, 1772.

Maria Elizabeth, daughter of Lewis Schneider, residing on the Hill, 6 months, 6 days old, died October 6, 1772, buried October 7, 1772.

Joseph, son of Henry Froelich, residing here in Germantown, 1 year, 2 months, 8 days old, died October 19, 1772, buried October 20, 1772.

John Rudolph, son of Conrad Zorn, 1 month, 6 days old, died November 6, 1772, buried November 8, 1772.

George Märcker, 14 years, 8 months, 12 days old, died December 17, 1772, buried December 18, 1772.

Catharine Bender, daughter of Joseph Bender, resident here, 2 months old, died December 29, 1772, December 30, 1772.

Maria Barbara Horter, 68 years, 13 days old, died December 3, 1772, buried January 1, 1773.

Catharine Mack, daughter of David Mack of Flourtown, 3 years, 6 months old, died January 4, 1775, buried January 5, 1775.

Anna Barbara Kehrbach, daughter of Jacob Kehrback, 3 years, 2 months, 1 day old, died January 4, 1775, buried January 5, 1775.

Charlotte Güterman, wife of Henry Gueterman, of Germantown, 32 years, 6 months, 7 days old, died January 15, 1775, buried January 17, 1775.

John Henry Albert, son of John Albert, of this place, 2 months, 8 days old, died January 21, 1775, buried January 22, 1775.

Elizabeth Benner, wife of John Benner of Germantown, 46 years, 1 month old, died January 25, 1775, buried January 26, 1775.

Joanna Eckert, daughter of John Eckart, 11 years, 11 months old, died January 28, 1775, buried January 29, 1775.

John Peter Campman, 70 years, 3 months, 3 days old, died February 25, 1775, buried February 27, 1775.

Joseph Bender, son of Joseph, 4 years, 3 months, 19 days, died February 28, 1775, buried March 2, 1775.

William Sommer, son of Jacob Sommer, 1 years, 1 month, 6 days old, died March 31, 1775, buried April 2, 1775.

Maria Sorber, daughter of Henry Sorber, 3 years, 6 months old, died April 4, 1775, buried April 6, 1775.

Anna Maria Wentzel, daughter of Philip Wentzel, 20 years, 2 months, 9 days old, died April 19, 1775, buried April 21, 1775.

Catharine Debus, wife of Albert Debus, 49 years old, died May 14, 1775, buried May 15, 1775.

Christine Lieser, daughter of Conrad Lieser, 1 year, 5 months, 23 days old, died June 26, 1775, buried June 27, 1775.

Elizabeth End, daughter of John End, 3 years, 9 months, 7 days old, died June 28, 1775, buried June 29, 1775.

John Bockius, son of Peter Bockius, 15 years, 10 months, 5 days old, died July 16, 1775, buried July 17, 1775.

Maria, daughter of Ulrich Freihoffer, shoemaker at Germantown, 1 year, 7 months old, died October 6, 1776, buried October 7, 1776.

Burials by Rev. Samuel Dubendorff, Easter 1777 - June 24, 1779

Frederick Fleckenstein, wagonmaker in Germantown, 47 years, 5 months, 6 days old, died January 6, 1777, buried January 9, 1777.

Henry Froelich, son of father of same name, 11 months old, died July 24, 1777, buried July 25, 1777.

Elizabeth, wife of Mr. Dost, nee Froelich, 39 years, 3 months, 2 days old, died August 1, 1777, buried August 3, 1777.

Anna Catharine, wife of Mr. Huegel, nee Schoen, 81 years, 1 month, 19 days old, died August 7, 1777, buried August 9, 1777.

Sarah, daughter of Abraham Gerster, of Frankfort, 1 year, 6 months, 10 days old, died August 21, 1777, buried August 23, 1777.

Bernard, son of Theobald End, of Germantown, 12 years, 8 months, 10 days old, died August 28, 1777, buried August 30, 1777.

Adam, son of Nicholas Schreiner, of Germantown, 1 year, 7 months, 11 days old, died September 5, 1777, buried September 6, 1777.

Maria Gertrude, wife of Mr. Laub, nee Moss, 45 years, 8 months, 11 days old, died September 13, 1777, September 14, 1777.

John Nuessle, of Frankfort, 89 years, 6 months old, died September 14, 1777, buried September 16, 1777.

John Adam Schuessler, of Flourtown, 68 years, 2 months, 2 days old, died December 19, 1777, December 21, 1777.

John Adolph, stockingweaver, Germantown, Lutheran, 45 years old, died December 31, 1777, buried January 1, 1778.

John George Braunsberg, of Bethelhausen, Lutheran, 54 years, 9 months, 3 days old, died January 4, 1778, buried January 6, 1778.

Anna Maria, wife of Mr. Hartranff, nee Busch, 22 years, 6 months, 6 days old, died January 7, 1778, buried January 9, 1778.

Henry Sorber, of Germantown, 28 years, 15 days old, died January 8, 1778, buried January 10, 1778.

Anna Catharine, wife of Mr. Huegel, married 54 years, 81 years, 6 months, 3 days old, died March 11, 1778, buried March 13, 1778.

Matthew Breiss, of Germantown, Lutheran, 62 years, 8 months old, died May 10, 1778, buried May 12, 1778.

Elizabeth Schuster, daughter of Petter Schuster, of Germantown, 18 years, 5 months, 3 days old, died September 8, 1778, buried September 9, 1778.

John Frederick Egersdorff, son of father of same name, Germantown, 7 years, 3 days old, died September 12, 1778, buried September 15, 1778.

Jacob Meier, son of Casper Meier, tawer, of Germantown, 1 year, 5 months, 20 days old, died September 25, 1778, buried September 26, 1778,

Maria Eva, daughter of Matthias Thiel, of Germantown, 10 months, 12 days old, died October 5, 1778, buried October 6, 1778.

Jacob Gottschalk, son of father of same name, Germantown, 2 years, 3 months old, died October 5, 1778, buried October 7, 1778.

John Dengel, citizen of Easton, died on his journey home, 58 years old, died October 9, 1778, buried October 11, 1778.

Barbara Christine, wife of Mr. Blecker, nee Pfaff, 60 years, 8

months old, died March 17, 1779, buried March 19, 1779.
Anna Elizabeth, daughter of Matthias Fering of Nicetown, 3 years, 7 months, 9 days old, died April 2, 1779, buried April 5, 1779.
Margaret, daughter of Daniel Campman, weaver, of Nicetown, 2 years, 1 month old, died April 7, 1779, buried April 9, 1779.
John Conrad Mack, stockingweaver, Germantown, age unknown, died April 9, 1779, buried April 10, 1779.
John Beier, son of father of same name, Germantown, 1 year, 7 months, 10 days old, died April 20, 1779, buried April 23, 1779.
Anna Cornelia Riess, widow, of Philadelphia, 71 years, 5 months old, died April 27, 1779, buried April 29, 1779.
Maria, daughter of Daniel Riess, stockingweaver, Germantown, 1 year, 10 months, 3 days old, died May 15, 1779, buried May 17, 1779.
Anna, daughter of Balthasar Heitrich, 3 years, 5 months, 8 days old, died May 22, 1779, buried May 23, 1779.
Regula Krauer, widow, 78 years, 2 months old, died June 12, 1779, buried June 13, 1779.

List of Deceased by Rev. Albert Helffenstein

George, son of Jacob Ritter, of Philadelphia, 9 months, 14 days old, died August 22, 1779, buried August 23, 1779.
Catharine Eisenmenger, single, Catholic, 57 years old, died August 28, 1779, buried August 29, 1779.
Anna Maria Reisinger, 66 years old, died September 3, 1779, buried Septemer 4, 1779.
Margaret Werner, 48 years, 4 months, 2 days old, died September 4, 179, buried September 5, 1779.
Anna Mayer, 68 years, 5 months old, died September 13, 1779, buried September 14, 1779.
Elizabeth Gertrude, daughter of Jacob Walcker, 4 months, 4 days old, died September 19, 1779, buried September 20, 1779.
Adam, son of John William Schneider, 10 years old, died September 21, 1779, buried September 22, 1779.
Margaret Faud, daughter of Jacob Faud and of his wife Louisa, 3 years, 5 months, 14 days old, died September 28, 1779, buried September 29, 1779.
Maria, daughter of Samuel Rosk and wife Christine, 4 years, 5 months, 16 days old, died October 16, 1779, buried October 17, 1779.
Anna Margaret Schuessler, 70 years, 6 months, 7 days old, died October 23, 1779, buried October 25, 1779.

Later burials of Mr. A. Helffenstein are missing. List of deceased, begun and continued by L. F. Hermann, p.t., 1790 -1799.

Albertus Helffenstein, pastor, 42 years, 3 months and some days old, died May 17, 1790, buried May 19, 1790.
Henry Krob, 85 years, 7 months, 8 days old, died October 27, 1790, buried October 29, 1790.
Christopher Henrici, 47 years, 3 months, 6 days old, died December 1, 1790, buried December 2, 1790.
Henry Gill, 65 years old, died December 22, 1790, buried December 25, 1790.

1791

John George Herrger, 80 years, 3 months, 20 days old, died January 26, 1791, buried January 28, 1791.

George, son of John Schmidt, 6 years, 3 months old, died January 28, 1791, buried January 30, 1791.

Catharine Gerbach, 27 years old, died February 7, 1791, buried February 9, 1791.

Catharien Dorothy Kerbach, 74 years, 4 months, 11 days old, died March 14, 1791, buried March 16, 1791.

Joseph David Grauer, 48 years, 3 months, 3 days old, died April 18, 1791, buried April 20, 1791.

Jacob, son of Jacob Dieder, 1 year, 4 months, 9 days old, died May 6, 1791, buried May 8, 1791.

Anna Magd., wife of Ludwig Amos, 70 years, 6 months, 19 days old, died May 2, 1791, buried May 4, 1791.

Simon Vogelgesang, 80 yrs old, d. May 17, 1791, bur. May 19, 1791.

John Kerbach, 57 years old, died May 28, 1791, buried May 30, 1791.

David Bley, 61 years old, died June 11, 1791, buried June 13, 1791.

Peter Bockius, a child, 8 months, 12 days old, died June 14, 1791, buried June 15, 1791.

Frederick Haffner's wife, 69 years old, died June 15, 1791, buried June 16, 1791.

Casper Hefft's child, 3 months old, died June 18, 1791, buried June 19, 1791.

Zacharias Simon, 61 years old, died July 16, 1791, buried July 17, 1791.

Jacob Klein, 69 years, 3 months, 24 days old, died August 2, 1791, buried August 4, 1791.

Henry Taylor, 43 years old, died August 12, 1791, buried August 13, 1791.

George, son of Jacob Staes, 9 years, 5 months, 2 days old, died September 1, 1791, buried September 3, 1791.

Jacob, son of Jacob Staes, 12 years less 7 days old, died September 7, 1791, buried September 9, 1791.

Fredeick, son of the Rev. Winkhaus and wife Catharine of Philadelphia, 1 year, 7 months, 11 days old, died September 9, 1791, buried September 11, 1791.

Jacob, son of Anthony Hergesheimer, 1 year, less 17 days old, died September 15, 1791, buried September 16, 1791.

Catharine, wife of George Haentz, 57 years, 6 months old, died September 17, 1791, buried September 18, 1791.

Anna Cath., daughter of Daniel Riess, 2 years, 3 days old, died September 18, 1791, buried September 20, 1791.

Rudolph, son of Jacob Maurer, 6 years, 6 months, 3 days old, died October 2, 1791, buried October 4, 1791.

Regina, daughter of John Fox, 4 years, 11 months, 7 days old, died October 7, 1791, buried October 9, 1791.

Louise Cath. Lehman, near Philadelphia, 62 years, 15 days old, died December 2, 1791, buried ----.

Charlotte, wife of Frederick Weinland, 21 years, 10 months old, died December 25, 1791, buried December 27, 1791.

Maria Magd. Hauser, Frankfort, 9 years, 2 months, 7 days old, died December 24, 1791, buried December 25, 1791.

Frederick Gerster, son of Fred. Gerster, Frankfort, 16 years, 3 months, 27 days old, died January 19, 1792, buried January 22,

1792.

John, son of Geo. Schuster, 2 years, 11 months old, died February 14, 1792, buried February 16, 1792.

Justus Schultz, son of Henry Schultz, 3 years, 5 months, 29 days old, died February 19, 1792, buried February 21, 1792.

Justa Christina Leibensetzer, nee Herman, 46 years, 9 days old, died April 7, 1792, buried April 9, 1792.

William Keyser, son of Henry Keyser, 8 years, 6 days old, died April 12, 1792, buried April 14, 1792.

John Beyl's wife, 54 years, 7 months old, died May 4, 1792, buried May 6, 1792.

Maria Louisa Metzler, widow, 62 years old, died May 6, 1792, buried May 8, 1792.

Jacob Loescher's child, 2 years old, died June 30, 1792, buried July 2, 1792.

Elizabeth, daughter of Felix Dettweiler, 37 years, 3 months, less 12 days old, died July 9, 1792, buried July 11, 1792.

Catharine Huhn, of Philadelphia, 29 years, 7 months, 16 days old, died July 21, 1792, buried July 22, 1792.

Andrew Gaemel, 65 years, 10 months, 7 days old, died August 1, 1792, buried August 3, 1792.

John Jaque Varnier, about 75 years old, died August 15, 1792, buried August 17, 1792.

Henry, son of Christian Vetter 3 months, 8 days old, died August 23, 1792, buried August 24, 1792.

Rachel, wife of Jacob Conrad, 81 years, 8 months, 9 days old, died September 13, 1792, buried September 15, 1792.

Philip, son of Rev. Philip Pauly and wife Elizabeth, of Whitpain, 4 years, 14 days old, died September 16, 1792, buried September 17, 1792.

Casper Geyer, Philadelphia, 65 years, 3 months, 14 days old, died September 17, 1792, buried September 18, 1792.

Joseph Flokrod, Frankfort, 28 years, 1 month old, died September 21, 1792, buried September 23, 1792.

Anna Maria, daughter of George Bressler, 2 years, 24 days old, died October 4, 1792, buried October 5, 1792.

John, son of Stevens Singlewood, 8 months, 14 days old, died November 1, 1792, buried November 2, 1792.

Daniel Paul, son of Abr. Paul of Bethelhausen, 35 years, 8 months, 1 day old, died November 13, 1792, buried November 15, 1792.

Jacob Haegy, 71 years, 2 months old, died November 23, 1792, buried November 25, 1792.

Magdalene, wife of George Richter, 42 years, 11 months, 7 days old, died December 31, 1792, buried January 2, 1793.

Margaret, daughter of John Bender, 15 years, 11 months, 24 days old, died January 11, 1793, buried January 13, 1793.

Peter Straub, 64 years, 10 months, 16 days old, died January 20, 1793, buried January 22, 1793.

Rudolph Puecky, 72 years, 1 month, 21 days old, died January 21, 1793 buried January 23, 1793.

Rudolph Guettinger, 74 years, 1 month, 24 days old, died February 19, 1793, buried February 21, 1793.

George Ihbuster, 82 years, 6 months, 23 days old, died February 24, 1793, buried February 26, 1793.

Anna Maria, daughter of Henry Leher, 2 years, 1 month, 10 days old,

died February 27, 1793, buried February 28, 1793.
George, son of Andrew Ceakler, 2 years, 6 months, 23 days old, died March 4, 1793, buried March 5, 1793.
Catharine, daughter of Joseph Bender, 18 years, 3 months, 17 days old, died March 5, 1793, buried March 7, 1793.
William Stuart, of Philadelphia, 28 years old, died May 11, 1793, buried May 13, 1792.
Mary Magdalene Schweitzer, of Philadelphia, 74 years, 6 months old, died May 16, 1793, buried May 18, 1793.
John Biconet, 68 years, 18 days old, died ----, buried ----.
Michael Kayser, 32 years, 8 months, 18 days old, died May 24, 1793, buried May 26, 1793.
Maria Yunker, 14 months old, died July 6, 1793, buried July 8, 1793.
Jacob Mayer, Frankfort, 57 years, 8 months, 24 days old, died July 8, 1793, buried July 10, 1793.
Rachel, daughter of George Benner, 17 years, 2 months, 15 days old, died July 12, 1793, buried July 14, 1793.
Polly, daughter of James Kahil, 4 years, 1 month, 4 days old, died July 15, 1793, buried July 17, 1793.
Susanna, daughter of Godfrey Bockius, 2 years, 2 months, 27 days old, died July 22, 1793, buried July 24, 1793.
David Stuardt, from New England, 22 years old, died July 27, 1793, buried July 28, 1793.
Peter, son of Rudolph Froely, 10 months, 4 days old, died August -, 1793, buried August 1, 1793.
Leonard Notz' child, 6 months, 27 days old, died August 1, 1793, buried August 2, 1793.
Henry Hickel's child, 4 years, less 4 days old, died August 10, 1793, buried August 11, 1793.
Jacob, son of Peter Vonringhaus, 4 years old, died August 13, 1793, buried August 14, 1793.
Valentine Koerbers, 4 months old, died August 13, 1793, buried August 15, 1793.
William, son of Henry Froely, 6 years 1 month, 5 days old, died August 25, 1793, buried August 28, 1793.
Dietrich Emig, 28 years, died August 27, 1793, buried August 28, 1793.
Jacob Neff, from Frankfort, 69 years, 7 months old, died September 27, 1793, buried September 29, 1793.
Jacob Herman Hein, from Bernhill, 74 years, 6 months, 19 days, died October 4, 1793, buried October 5, 1793.
Anna Barbara, daughter of Henry Sorber, 6 months, 7 days, died October 4, 1793, buried October 5, 1793.
Henry Schuetz, Sen., 51 years, 5 months, 7 days old, died October 7, 1793, buried October 8, 1793.
Henry Hinkel, a child, 2 years, 6 months, 17 days old, died October 16, 1793, buried October 17, 1792.
Sebastian, son of Godfrey Bockius, 6 years, 5 months, 17 days old, died October 25, 1793, buried October 27, 1793.
John Beyls, 66 years, 3 months, 17 days old, died October 27, 1793, buried October 28, 1793.
Susanna, daughter of Henry Froely, 2 years, 3 months, 6 days old, died October 28, 1793, buried October 29, 1793.
Maria Margaret Lang, widow, 70 years, 1 month old, died November 1,

1793, buried November 3, 1793.
John Gartner, 70 years, 3 months, 10 days old, died November 21, 1793, buried November 27, 1793.
John, son of Andrew Rigler, 11 months, 11 days old, died ----, 1793, buried ----, 1793.
John Schneider, 83 years, 2 months, 9 days old, died December 28, 1793, buried December 30, 1793.
Dewald End, 86 years, 4 months, 14 days old, died January 11, 1794, buried January 14, 1794.
Magdalene Rohrer, Frankfort, 78 years, 2 days old, died January 28, 1794, buried January 30, 1794.
Catharine Schlatter, 19 years, 11 months old, died February 1, 1794, buried February 2, 1794.
Philippina Catharine Bockius, daughter of Francis Bockius, 15 years, 10 months, 11 days old, died February 13, 1794, buried February 16, 1794.
Jacob Froely, Dr. Med., 38 years, 1 month, 20 days old, died February 25, 1794, buried February 26, 1794.
---- Kuntzy, ---- old, died March --, 1794, buried March --, 1794.
Susanna De Dieur, widow, 73 years old, died March 9, 1794, buried March 11, 1794.
Ulrich Schlatter's son, 7 months old, died March 23, 1794, buried March 25, 1794.
Leonard Steinbrenner, 76 years, 7 months, 6 days old, died June 17, 1794, buried June 18, 1794.
Daniel Groeninger, 83 years, 3 months, 2 days old, died June 26, 1794, buried June 27, 1794.
John Endt, 60 years old, died ----, 1794, buried ----, 1794.
Hannah, daughter of Henry Schermer, 11 months, 23 days old, died October 28, 1794, buried October 29, 1794.
Nicholas Michael Vence, *natif de Marseille en Provence*, 36 years old, died November 9, 1794, buried November 11, 1794.
Peter Bleckert's child, 1 year, 10 months, 18 days old, died November 21, 1794, buried November 22, 1794.
Henry, son of Henry Sorber, 6 years, 2 months, 18 days old, died December 20, 1794, buried December 21, 1794.
Anna Riester, 63 years old, died December 4, 1794, buried December 5, 1794.
Maria Trong, 65 years, 3 days old, died December 25, 1794, buried December 26, 1794.
Anna Reiss, widow of Daniel Reiss, 59 years old, died January 15, 1795, buried January 17, 1795.
Mary Weidman, 75 years old, died ----, 1795, buried ----, 1795.
Thomas Dongan's son, 48 months old, died February 22, 1795, buried February 25, 1795.
William Dosten, 1 year, 2 months old, died ----, 1795, buried ----, 1795.
Charles Benville, D.M., 69 years, 11 months, 6 days old, died March 17, 1795, buried March 19, 1795.
Samuel, son of Henry Behr, 1 year, 5 months, 9 days old, died April 12, 1795, buried April 13, 1795.
John Mann's son, 21 years old, died July --, 1795, buried July --, 1795.
George Bressler, 5 months, 11 days old, died July 9, 1795, buried

July 10, 1795.

Joseph, son of Benjamin Paul, 1 year, 6 months, 13 days old, died July 19, 1795, buried July 20, 1795.

Jacob, son of David Marshall, 1 year, 3 months, 1 day old, died July 26, 1795, buried July 27, 1795.

John Engle, 74 years old, died July 26, 1795, buried July 27, 1795.

Elizabeth Landenberger, 3 months, 12 days old, died July 30, 1795, buried July 31, 1795.

Henry Gilbert's child, 10 months, 22 days old, died August 1, 1795, buried August 2, 1795.

William, son of Peter Miller, 8 months, 1 day old, died August 3, 1795, buried August 4, 1795.

John Schuster's child, 14 years, 6 months, 18 days old, died August 9, 1795, buried August 10, 1795.

Mary, daughter of Adam Becker, 18 years, 1 day old, died August 9, 1795, buried August 10, 1795.

John Rudolph, son of Adam Becker, 2 years, 19 days old, died August 14, 1795, buried August 16, 1795.

Elizabeth, wife of John Barral, 23 years, 5 days old, died ----, 1795, buried ----, 1795.

Jacob Behr, 21 years, 8 months, 8 days old, died September 1, 1795, buried September 2, 1795.

Rudolph Guettinger's widow, 75 years old, died ----, 1795, buried ----, 1795.

Christian Gutknecht, 73 years, 6 months, 2 days old, died December 26, 1795, buried December 27, 1795.

Edmund R. Herman, 1 year, 4 months, 10 days old, died November 3, 1795, buried November 4, 1795.

Daniel, son of John Weil, 2 years, 1 month, 8 days old, died January 7, 1796, buried January 8, 1796.

John McFell's son, 4 months, 26 days old, died February 6, 1796, buried February 7, 1796.

George, son of Justus Schuetz, 6 months, 1 day old, died February 6, 1796, buried February 8, 1796.

Sam. Neswinger's wife, Frankfort, 74 years old, died February 13, 1796, buried February 14, 1796.

John Endt, 29 years, 5 months, 16 days old, died February 18, 1796, buried February 20, 1796.

Elizabeth Bliss, 3 years, 8 months old, died February 24, 1796, buried February 25, 1796.

John Ernst's child, 2 months, 4 days old, died March 14, 1796, buried March 15, 1796.

Cath. Stadelman, 16 years, 7 months, 3 days old, died ----, 1796, buried ----, 1796.

Jacob Gerster's wife Sophia, 43 years, 13 days old, died May 9, 1796, buried May 10, 1796.

Widow of Francis Thiel, 75 years, 2 days old, died May 7, 1796, buried May 8, 1796.

Anna Barbara, widow of Simon Vogelgesang, 75 years, 6 months, 1 day old, died ----, 1796, buried ----, 1796.

John Hink's daughter, 14 years old, died June 26, 1796, buried June 26, 1796.

George Schuster's child, 9 months, 3 days old, died ----, 1796, buried July 1, 1796.

Margaret Landenberger, 1 month, 10 days old, died July 6, 1796,

buried July 7, 1796.
John Mayer's daughter, 3 years, 5 months old, died July 10, 1796, buried July 11, 1796.
John Drong's son, 1 year, 9 months 7 days old, died July 11, 1796, buried July 13, 1796.
Catharine Peters, 12 years old, died July 13, 1796, buried July 14, 1796.
Henry, son of Justus Schuetz, 11 months, 15 days old, died July 17, 1796, buried July 19, 1796.
Christopher Ottinger's child, 1 year, 4 months, 25 days old, died July 26, 1796, buried July 27, 1796.
Archibold Engel, Philadelphia, 37 years old, died July 30, 1796, buried July 31, 1796.
Jacob Weidman's child, 7 years, 3 months, 4 days old, died August 13, 1796, buried August 14, 1796.
Frederick, son of Henry Gerster, 1 year, 3 months, 24 days old, died August 13, 1796, buried August 15, 1796.
Jacob Miller's child, 1 year, 9 months, 24 days old, died August 17, 1796, buried August 18, 1796.
Jacob Weidman's child, 3 years old, died August 18, 1796, buried August 19, 1796.
Henry Maurer's wife, Frankfort, 23 years, 6 months old, died August 19, 1796, buried August 20, 1796.
Godfrey Dearfille's daughter, 3 years old, died August 19, 1796, buried August 20, 1796.
Philip Braun's child, 1 year old, died September 3, 1796, buried September 4, 1796.
Jacob Unrath's wife, 46 years, 6 months old, died September 28, 1796, buried September 30, 1796.
Magdalene, wife of Jacob Horter, 61 years, 9 months old, died December 1, 1796, buried December 2, 1796.
George Miller, 67 years, 1 month, 11 days old, died January 8, 1797, buried January 9, 1797.
Balthasar Roth, 46 years old, died January 30, 1797, buried February 1, 1797.
George Hinks, ---- old, died ----, 1797, buried ----, 1797.
Anna Margaret Rohrman, 31 years, 13 days old, died March 29, 1797, buried March 30, 1797.
John Miller, 62 years old, died March 31, 1797, buried April 1, 1797.
Hester Devis, 2 years old, died ----, 1797, buried ----, 1797.
Elizabeth Young, 3 years old, died ----, 1797, buried ----, 1797.
John Man's child, 8 months, 18 days old, died ----, 1797, buried ----, 1797.
Elizabeth Hoens, 4 months, 24 days old, died ----, 1797, buried ----, 1797.
Mr. Jones' child, 1 year old, died ----, 1797, buried ----, 1797.
Martin Wentzel's child, 7 months old, died ----, 1797, buried ----, 1797.
Mr. Dourfille's child, about 2 years old, died ----, 1797, buried ----, 1797.
William Schmid's child, 11 months old, died ----, 1797, buried ---, 1797.
Conrad Ax's child, ---- old, died ----, 1797, buried ----, 1797.
Susan Fox, 3 years, 18 days old, died ----, 1797, buried ----,

1797.

William, son of Jacob Weidman, 8 months old, died ----, 1797, buried ----, 1797.

John Maurer's child, 2 years, 8 months old, died ----, 1797, buried ----, 1797.

John Landenberger's child, 2 months old, died September 5, 1797, buried September 6, 1797.

Abraham Paul's child, ---- old, died ----, 1797, buried ----, 1797.

---- Giebler's child, ---- old, died ----, 1797, buried ----, 1797.

Henry Bergy, 76 years, 10 months, 19 days old, died November 30, 1797, buried December 3, 1797.

George Kerster, 87 years, 9 months, 17 days old, died December 24, 1797, buried December 26, 1797.

John Haentz's child, 7 months, 4 days old, died December 25, 1797, buried December 27, 1797.

Peter Schrank's wife, 56 years, 8 months, 21 days old, died December 29, 1797, buried December 30, 1797.

Elizabeth Bender, 20 years, 10 months old, died January 2, 1798, buried January 3, 1798.

William Kirk, 20 years, 4 months old, died January 12, 1798, buried January 13, 1798.

William Stevenson, 5 years, 10 months, 24 days old, died February 16, 1798, buried February 17, 1798.

Michael Schmidt's wife, 65 years old, died March 4, 1798, buried March 5, 1798.

Henry Schnabel, 50 years old, died March 21, 1798, buried March 22, 1798.

Anna Margaret Schnabel, 74 years old, died March 30, 1798, buried March 31, 1798.

Benjamin Paul, 2 months old, died May 6, 1798, buried May 7, 1798.

John Kessler, 50 years, 10 months old, died May 17, 1798, buried May 18, 1798.

Catharine, daughter of Jacob Duy, 8 months, 13 days old, died June 1, 1798, buried June 3, 1798.

Jaques's wife, 47 years old, died July 3, 1798, buried July 4, 1798.

Jacob Dietrich's child, 9 months old, died July 4, 1798, buried July 5, 1798.

Bernard Schucker's child, 5 months, 11 days old, died July 16, 1798, buried July --, 1798.

Mr. N. N. in Mr. Hochlander's house, 35 years old, died July 26, 1798, buried July 27, 1798.

Shoemaker's child, 1 year old, died July 27, 1798, buried July 28, 1798.

John Corwell's child, 1 year, 4 months old, died July 27, 1798, buried July 28, 1798.

James Hendersons, 1 year, 5 months old, died July 30, 1798, buried July 31, 1798.

J. Schuster's son, 19 years old, died December --, 1798, buried December 2, 1798.

Rev. Dr. Hendel, 57 years, 10 months, 6 days old, funeral sermon in the church at Philadelphia, died September 26, 1798, buried December 9, 1798.

G. King's daughter, 14 years old, died ----, 1798, buried December 23, 1798.

Maria Elizabeth Dannehauer, 84 years old, died January 12, 1799, buried January 13, 1799.
Jacob Engel, 71 years, 8 months, 23 days old, died February 19, 1799, buried February 21, 1799.
John Keyser, 78 years old, died March 2, 1799, buried March 8, 1799.
Michael Lange's son, 1 month, 2 days old, died March 2, 1799, buried March 3, 1799.
Anna Maria Christina Wentzel, 74 years, 6 months, 21 days old, died April 10, 1799, buried April 11, 1799.
John Merten, in Whitpain, 77 years, 10 months, 9 days old, died March 6, 1799, buried March 8, 1799.
Anthony Bygony, 35 years, 1 month, 2 days old, died April 14, 1799, buried April 16, 1799.
Robert Cornwell, 52 years, 3 months, 22 days old, died April 22, 1799, buried April 29, 1799.
Catharine Gotwald, 85 years, less 11 days old, died April 30, 1799, buried May 3, 1799.
Anna White, 73 years, 1 month, 5 days old, died May 17, 1799, buried May 18, 1799.
Elizabeth, daughter of Godfrey Dorfille, 1 year, 2 months old, died May 17, 1799, buried May 18, 1799.

[No other deaths are recorded through 1800.]

CATECHUMENS

By J. G. Alsentz:
Pentecost, 1758
Jacob Mayer, 17 years
John Rausch, 17 years, 4 months
Daniel Ries, 14 years
Elizabeth Froelig, 19 years, 1 month
Maria Eliz. Kern 18 years, 9 months
Anna Christine Kampmann, 18 years, 3 months
Anna Meyer, 17 years, 1 month
Elizabeth Von der Linden, 16 years, 10 months
Barbara Waltzener, 15 years, 10 months
Cath. Elizab. Nollerd, 15 years, 8 months
Maria Eliz. Nissli, 15 years, 5 months
Maria Eliz. Zimmerle, 14 years, 4 months

Easter Day, 1759:
Peter Staud, about 25 years
Jacob Meyer, 24 years
Henry Rummer, about 18 years
Michael Mischot, about 19 years
Jacob Gardner, 19 years
Christopher Weidman, 17 years
Rudolph Grauer, 17 years, 11 months
Lewis Grauer, 14 years, 3 months
Henry Froelig, 15 years
Henry Simon, 16 years
Peter Edeborn, 16 years
Abraham Miller, 15 years, 4 months
Anna Maria Miller, 18 years
Agnes Rau, 18 years
Barbara Sorber, 17 years
Anna Barbara Jung, 16 years, 6 months
Margaret Mootz, 15 years
Elizabeth Halach, 14 years
Margaret, wife of Henry Mercke, ---- Bartholomae

Good Friday, April 4, 1760:
Andrew Weber, married, about 23 years
Henry Schuetz, 18 years
Valentine Hang, 16 years

John von der Linden, 15 years
Henry Mayer, 15 years
Matthew Rausch, 15 years
Matthew Marten, 14 years
Gertrude Klaus, 19 years
Elizabeth Rohrer, 18 years
Anna Maria Dedier, 17½ years
Susanna Hess, 16 years, 9 months
Hester Madery, 16 years, 3 months
Elizabeth Bleckler, 15 years, 3 months
Margaret Groskopp, 15 years
Margaret Vay, 16 years, 6 months
Charlotte Gensel, 15 years
Anna Maria Thoes, 14 years

Good Friday, March 20, 1761:
Jacob Wuertz, 24 years
Frederick Gerster, 21 years
George Gerster, 23 years
Jacob Gerster, 19 years
John Weydman, 16 years
Henry Summer, 21 years
Peter Weckerle, 19 years
Jacob Saenger, 16 years
Christopher Groskopp, 15 years
Veronica Angst, 20 years
Catharine Froely, 18 years, 6 months
Sarah Login, 20 years
Anna Maria Knisel, 18 years, 8 months
Susanna Dedier, 18 years, 6 months
Veronica Miller, 17 years
Susanna Angst, 17 years
Maria Elizabeth Login, 16 years, 3 months
Anna Margaret Schiebely, 17 years
Anna Maria Hoffman, 16 years
Maria Eliz. Gerster, 16 years
Anna Elizabeth Knisel, 16 years
Eva Margaret Streby, 16 years
Catharine Simon, 15 years, 6 months
Elizabeth Ernst, 15 years
Maria Waltzener, 15 years
Catharine Koller, 14 years
Regina Nisle, -- years

March 31, 1763:
Frederick Schmick, 22 years
John Peter Dedier, 18 years
Frederick Schuebely, 18 years
Theodore Grosskopp, 15 years
Nicholas Rausch, 16 years
Henry Mayer, 17 years
Peter Backofen, 20 years
Samuel Runckel
Lawrence Remig
Conrad Becker
Maria Wollbach, 19 years
Anna Maria Joost, 18 years
Elizabeth Trimber, 18 years
Catharine Angst, 17 years
Catharine Bickes, 17 years
Anna Maria Hange, 16 years
Veronica Mayer, 16 years
Catharine Rivert, 15 years, 6 months
Barbara Simon, 15 years
Maria Zimmerle, 15 years
Margaret Berky, 14 years
Anna Maria Hegely, married
Anna Maria Bumm

April 20, 1764:
Henry Dischong, 22 years
Frederick Dischong, 20 years
Carl Pein, 15 years
Casper Weitzel, 15½ years
John Froely, 16 years
Benjamin Schuetz, 14 years, 2 months
Paul Groskopp, 14 years, 6 months
Elizabeth Fritschy, 17 years
Veronia Summer, 19 years
Maria Collman, 18 years
Barbara Wentz, 18 years
Maria Hoffmann, 18 years
Joanna Mayer, 18 years, 10 months
Maria Agnes Petry, 16 years
Susanna Koenig, 17 years, 9 months
Catharine Summer, 16½ years
Catharine Collman, 15 years
Margaret Ries, 14 years
Barbara Bickes, 15 years
Elizabeth Steitz, 13½ years

June 9, 1764:
Elizabeth Kohler, 23 years
Elizabeth Hoffmann, 16 years

Catharine Dueppel, 15 years
Catharine Clages, 17 years
Maria Morris, 23 years
Catharine Zacharias, 15 years, 11 months
Sophia Leipkap, 18 years
Catharine Haas, 16 years, 6 months

Easter and Pentecost 1765:
Jacob van der Lind, 17 years
Peter Schuch, 23 years
John Drachsel, 16 years
Catharine Gaerdner, 15 years, 7 months
Catharine Joergin, 14 years
Cath. von der Lind, 14 years
Elizabeth Simon, 16 years
Catharine Lefaeber, 17 years
Maria Angst, 17 years
Sarah Walther, 20 years
Anna Barbara Deschler, 16 years
Susanna Schuster, 16 years
Catharine Elk, 15 years, 4 months
Elizabeth Gaerdner, 14 years, 3 months
Maria Barbara Drachsel, 14 years, 8 months

Easter 1766:
John Wentz, 21 years
Joseph Linckenhauer, 20 years
Christian Knorr, 17 years
William Hirsch, 16 years
Mathew Zimmerle, 18 years
John George Eters, 18 years
Jacob Knisel, 16 years
John Saenger, 16 years
John Eters, 15 years
Daniel Bechtely, 15 years
Adam Schneider, 15 years
Henry Summerauer, 15 years
Henry Krum, 16 years
Christian Krum, 16 years
Nicholas Colman, 15 years
Catharine Ernst, 22 years
Elizabeth Ernst, 19 years
Margaret Welker, 18 years
Anna Catharine Schubely, 18 years
Anna Barbara Weydner, 17 years
Margaret Eters, 16 years
Susanna Berki, 15 years
Catharine Freury, 17 years
Catharine Mayer, 15 years
Eva Schneider, 15 years
Maria Bechtely, 17 years
Eva Elizabeth Frank, 20 years
Catharine Hartmann, 16 years
Anna Neuschwanger, 15 years
Anna Margaret Knorr, 15 years
Maria Lehmann, 16 years, 9 months
Margaret Dippel, 15 years
Elizabeth Klages, 17 years
Elizabeth Martin, 14 years, 8 months
Maria Faust, 14 years, 4 months
Catharine Schaufelberger, 17 years
Margaret Hange, 18 years
Catharine Knisel, 18 years
Elizabeth Beil, 14 years

1768 by John Christopher Faber, Vicar:
John Bockius, 19 years
William Bockius, 17 years
Andrew Dauber, 17 years
John Klages, 15 years
Henry Jung, 16 years
John Schiblieu, 17 years
Nicholas Statt, 15 years
Michael Simon, 16 years
George Mayer, 24 years
Catharine Froelich, 14 years
Catharine Stat, 18 years
Magdalene Bettilion, 15 years
Susanna Ernst, 16 years
Sophia Ernst, 15 years
Elizabeth Gutknecht, 15 years
Susanna Goetting, 15 years
Anna Goetting, 16 years
Anna Catharine Metzler, 17 years
Anna Maria Jung, 15 years

May 12, 1769, by Rev. Christian Frederick Foehring:
Henry Ernst, 20 years, 9 months
Henry Tenig, 16 years
Catharine Kruess, 19 years
Veronica Witeman, 16 years
Susanna Gardner, 16 years
Maria Gardner, 15 years
Barbara Tenig, 15 years
Elizabeth Coleman, 16 years
Regina Bingeman, 17 years
Anna Conrad, 18 years

April 13, 1770:
Henry Sorber, 20 years
Peter Simons, 16 years
Casper Maier, 18 years
George Wonner, 17 years
Abraham Henry, 16 years
Philip Conrad, 23 years
John Meier, 16 years
Jacob Geisel, 17 years
Franciscus Bockius, 16 years
Peter Schuster, 18 years
Paul Schuster, 16 years
Charles Deschler, 15 years
Joseph Painter
Andrew Barnerd
Jacob Conrad, 21 years
Anna Keller, 18 years
Barbara Gittinger, 15 years
Elsie Rohrer, 16 years
Catharine Long, 15 years
Rosina Hess, 13 years
Susanna Haus, 16 years
Barbara Solomon, 19 years
Christina Bleker, 16 years
Maria Barb. Falconer, 13 years
Barbara Summer, 16 years
Sarah Geisel, 15 years
Catharine Brown, 16 years
Margaret Metzler, 18 years
Sophia Rederbach, 18 years
Rosina Rederbach, 16 years
Catharine Edeborn 27 years
Catharine Hammer
Maria Hammer

March 29, 1771:
Philip Bornhueter, 16 years
Joseph Kemmel, 19 yers
John Dudweiler, 17 years
Joseph Dearman, 19 years
George Kornman, 18 years
John Henry Schneider, 14 years
Jacob Weber, 18 years
Elias Peter, 16 years
George Miller, 21 years
Barbara Sorber, 19 years
Christine Werner, 18 years
Anna Eliz. Bickes, 16 years
Barbara Marker
Maria Fries, 15 years
Elizabeth Dudweiler, 16 years
Catharine Summerlath, 16½ years
Christine Groff, 15 years
Eva Gardner, 14 years
Hannah Coler, 16 years

April 7, 1772:
Rudolph Froelich, 15 years, 9 months
Christian Gutknecht, 16 years
John Schuster, 17 years
Philip Riffert, 15 years
Catharine Schaeffer, 15 years
Maria Eliz. Henry, 15 years
Anna Jung, 16 years
Elizabeth Weidtman, 14 years
Henry Vanderlin, 15 years
William Hegy, 15 years, 6 months
Andrew Kemmel, 18 years, 2 months
Michael Reifschneider, 21 years
John Peter, 17 years, 8 months
John Peiffer
Solomon Sells
Maria Vetter, 17 years
Elizabeth Raderbach, 16 years
Elizabeth Brown, 14 years
Catharine Hess, 14 years
Maria Riffert, 14 years
Maria Sorber, 14 years
Margaret Sells, 15 years
Margaret Schuster, 15 years
Elizabeth Amos, 16 years
Catharine Neschler, 15 years
Elizabeth Smith, 16 years
Susanna Barringer, 16 years

Easter 1773, by Rev. J.C. Albert Helffenstein:
Godfrey Bockius, 15 years, 5 months
Joseph Mueller, 16 years, 2 months
Michael Becker, 15 years
Susanna Mueller, 17 years
Margaret Bockius, 16 years
Magdalene Schmid, 15 years
Anna Maria Wentzel, 15 years
Anna Maria Reemer, 16 years
Anna Elizabeth Stal, 15 years
Elizabeth Schaecke, 16 years

Easter 1774:
Leonard Gund, 17 years
John Ernst Riess, 15 years, 8 months
John Wentzel, 16 years, 7 months
John Sorber, 17 years, 3 months
Carl Schuster, 16 years, 7

months
Andrew Schuster, 16 years, 7 months
John Jacob Staud, 15 years
Philip Coleman, 16 years, 6 months
Christian Geissel, 16 years
Philp Friess, 16 years
Barbara Eubester, 17 years
Catharine Horder, 16 years
Elizabeth Essig, 17 years
Anna Barbara Merck, 17 years

Easter 1775:
Peter Froelich, 16 years, 3 months
Jacob Meng, 19 years
Leonard Sommer, 17 years
John Kolman, 16 years, 1 month
Henry Essig, 15 years, 3 months
William York, 15 years, 6 months
John Ebrecht, 17 years, 1 month
John Schmidt, 16 years, 5 months
Valentine Wunner, 17 years
Valentine Schmidt, 16 years
Isaac Betillion, 16 years, 8 months
Andrew Hess, 15 years
John Lehman, 16 years, 9 months
Lawrence Riess, 15 years
Dorothy Meng, 17 years, 6 months
Deborah Froelich, 22 years
Mary Magdalene Daubert, 17 years, 6 months
Salome Miller, 15 years
Anna Maria Huhn, 16 years, 3 months
Christine Ebrecht, 15 years, 3 months
Rachel Conrad, 18 years, 5 months
Margaret Ebrecht, 19 years, 2 months
Elizabeth Schuster, 15 years, 1 months
Maria Catharine Bockius, 15 years, 10 months
Maria Van der Weil, 17 years, 5 months

(On account of the long vacancy and the confusion of the war, no reports are in existence of the children confirmed in the years 1776, 1777 and 1778. - Note of the Rev. Samuel Dubendorff.)

Easter 1779, by Rev. Samuel Dubendorf:
Henry Ernst, 18 years
Balthasar Ernst, 16 years
John Schaefer
John Bornhueter
David Michele
Jacob Sorber, 19 years
Samuel Gutknecht
Magdalene Ernst, 15 years
Margaret Straub
Anna Straub
Elizabeth Heinrich
Veronica Staat
Catharine Lang, 19 years
Elizabeth Koerber, 18 years
Barbara Kuebler, 16 years
Anna Barbara Sorber, 17 years
Magdalene Wentzel

Pentecost 1779:
Henry Sorber
Mrs. Elizabeth Wentzel, nee Wasselman

Pentecost 1780:
George Miller, 19 years
Jacob Miller, 18 years
William End, 16 years
Jacob Rummel, 17 years
Samuel Diehl, 16 years
Henry Dettweiler, 20 years
George Schmid, 19 years
Benjamin Weber, 17 years
Jacob Edenborn, 17 years
Henry Haendel, 16 years
John Schreiner, 15 years
John Piquone, 18 years
Christian Hess, 16 years
Joseph Sorber, 16 years
Jacob Mayer, 19 years
John Froelich, 19 years
Werner Mayer, 18 years
Ludwig Bender, 16 years
Joseph Piquone, 21 years
Daniel End, 22 years
Catharine Rummel, 16 years
Catharine Sorber, 18 years
Margaret Renacher, 19 years

Susanna Scheddinger, 20 years
Elizabeth Schmid, 18 years
Elizabeth Schlatter, 17 years
Maria Neracher, 18 years
Elizabeth Hausman, 15 years
Barbara Wunner, 17 years
Anna Bickes, 17 years
Maria Maurer, 17 years
Elizabeth Maurer, 15 years
Anna Froelich, 18 years
Dorothy Matthes, 16 years
Catharine Marg. Jacob, 16 years
Elizabeth Miller, 15 years
Maria Kraemer, 15 years
Margaret Diehl, 30 years
Margaret Keller, 18 years
Catharine Piquone, 17 years
Catharine Muth, 18 years
Anna Mayer, 17 years

April 22, 1791, of Rev. L. Frederick Herman:
Henry Born
Joseph Kibler
Frederick Kerber
Peter Haentz
Elizabeth Jacob
Anna Hinkel
Barbara Bockly
Margaret Bernhueter
Louise Haentz
Maria Heidrick
John Michael Hopp, 23 years
Jacob Guth, a married man who was baptized at the same time.
George Bressler, from Nicetown, a married man

April 8, 1792:
Henry Gardner
John Kampman
Conrad Behr
Fred. Staudt
Joseph Bockius
Henry Hues
Maria Froelich
Maria Mohr
Christine Berger
Elizabeth Bingert
Elizabeth Froelich
Catharine Bender
Maria Haentz
Christine Grosskopf
Margaret Schuetz
Maria Weber, now Rose
Elizabeth Lamb, now Nutz
Elizabeth Braun
Salome Staehs
Mrs. Susanna Wummersdorff, 67 years

On August 3, (1792) the Holy Communion was administered to Mr. George Friess in his house because he was sick.

On September 24, 1792 the Holy Communion was given to the old Mr. Lochner, of Frankfort, here in my home.

On February 28, 1793 the Holy Communion was given to the wife of John Staer, at Bethelhausen, on her sickbed.

March 29, 1793:
Godfrey Hoffman
Michael Straub
Peter Kessler
Anna Unrath
Elizabeth Unrath
Anna Schuetz
Regina Straub
Maria Emis
Hannah Kerber
Sarah Notz
Christine Notz

On August 20, 1793, the Holy Communion was given to the widow Catharine Hertzel, living in the poorhouse at Germantown.

April 18, 1794:
Henry Jacob
John Grosskoph
Matthew Miller

Abraham Eberhard
Peter Kolp
George Endt
Jacob Mayer
Margaret Gilbert
Sybilla Endt
Maria Eberhardt
Elizabeth Bender
Maria Kehl
Catharine Gardner
Catharine Stehs
Elizabeth Miller

Easter 1795:
Peter Dedier
Conrad Harris
Wm. Ross

John Gilbert
Wm. Notz
Henry Schettinger
John Lenhard
George Lenhard
Catharine Deal
Anna Weidman
Elizabeth Hinkel
Eva Ottinger

Easter 1796:
Sally Schuetz
Elizabeth Fein

On January 8, 1797, upon her hearty desire, the communion was administered to the mother-in-law of Abraham Kerber, who resided with him in his home, since, because of age and weakness, she was unable to attend the communion on Christmas Day.

On January 9, 1797 the aged Mr. Roth, living on the land of Mr. Schumacher in Germantown, received the Communion upon his sickbed.

Good Friday, April 14, 1797:
Jacob Hagy
Leonard Strieber
George Notz
George Hoffman
William Emis
Samuel Weber
John Dedier
George Friess
Elizabeth Schneider
Maria Guebler
Sally Weber
Charlotte Dedier

Pentecost 1797:
Mrs. Elizabeth Hantz

On November 13, 1797 the aged Henry Bergy received the Holy Communion at his request on his sickbed.

On November 16, (1797) the aged Mrs. Dannehauer received the Communion on her sickbed.

December 25, 1797:
John Kunius

Good Friday 1798:
Henry Rohrer
Jonathan Leonhard
Daniel Dappen
George Schukerd
John Bockius
John Kerper
Frederick Kerper
Elizabeth Freitag
Catharine Kerper
Mary Geissel
Barbara Bockius
Catharine Grosskopf
Susanna Freind
Hetty Meyer
Peggy Meyer

Easter 1798:
John Engel, married

Good Friday 1799:
George Hoffman
Jacob Staudt
George Schneider
Charlotte Notz
Mary Hagy, now Sutter
Mary Streber
Elizabeth Schneider

Sally Harris
Catharine Bockius
Catharine Kessler
Elizabeth Henk
Mary Magdalene Feyn

Pentecost, June 8, 1802, by Rev. William Runkel:
John Runkel, 17 years
Joseph Osias, 19 years
Henry Lehnhard, 16 years
Daniel Strieper, 17 years
Peter Goetz, 20 years
Christian Kolbe, married, 24 years
Henry Werffel, married, 25 years
John Kiely, 18 years
Geo. Kiely, 17 years
Michael Shauer, 19 years
Barbara Notz, 16 years
Magdalene Kolbe, 18 years
Elizabeth Kolbe, 15 years
Margaret Freyhoffer, 17 years
Anna Schnabel, 16 years
Susanna Osias, 17 years
Maria Schuchard, 17 years
Maria Sorber, 17 years
Elizabeth Kerper, 18 years
Maria Lehnhard, 17 years
Barbara Stehs, 18 years
Maria Stehs, 15 years
Marg. Rohrer, 16 years
Maria Schuster, 18 years
Barbara Schuster, 18 years
Eliz. Fehring, 17 years
Cath. Schauer, 17 years
Marg. Brunner, 19 years

April 8, 1803:
Christian Wunder, 20 years
Michael Unruh, 23 years
George Unruh, 21 years
William Unruh, 18 years
William Wunder, 21 years
John Wentzel, 21 years
George Miller, 18 years
Joseph Jacob, 18 years
Catharine Runkel, 16 years
Maria Bockius, 16 years
Catharine Schinkel, 18 years
Margaret Baer, 17 years
Margaret Kampman, 18 years
Maria Steger, 17 years
Dorothea Wentzel, 16 years
Elizabeth Wentzel, 17 years
Rachel Miller, 17 years
Elizabeth Peters, 19 years
Marg. Diel, 16 years
Elizabeth Gilbert, 20 years
Sarah Gilbert, 17 years
Anna Keiser, 16 years
Anna Bockius, 16 years

INDEX

-C-

-H-

www.ingramcontent.com/pod-product-compliance
Lightning Source LLC
LaVergne TN
LVHW050649100826
845148LV00011B/2052

* 9 7 8 0 7 8 8 4 2 5 9 8 1 *